DARE

TO WEAR YOUR

Soul

ON THE OUTSIDE

ALSO BY GLORIA J. BURGESS

Books

Legacy Living: The Six Covenants for Personal & Professional Excellence
Continuum: The First Songbook of Sweet Honey in the Rock (editor)

Poetry

Journey of the Rose
The Open Door

DARE
TO WEAR YOUR
Soul
ON THE OUTSIDE

Live Your Legacy Now

Gloria J. Burgess

Foreword by Angeles Arrien

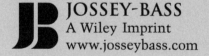

JOSSEY-BASS
A Wiley Imprint
www.josseybass.com

Published by Jossey-Bass
A Wiley Imprint
989 Market Street, San Francisco, CA 94103-1741—www.josseybass.com

Credits appear on p. 232

Readers should be aware that Internet Web sites offered as citations and/or sources for further
information may have changed or disappeared between the time this was written and when it is read.

Limit of Liability/Disclaimer of Warranty: While the publisher and author have used their best efforts
in preparing this book, they make no representations or warranties with respect to the accuracy
or completeness of the contents of this book and specifically disclaim any implied warranties of
merchantability or fitness for a particular purpose. No warranty may be created or extended by sales
representatives or written sales materials. The advice and strategies contained herein may not be
suitable for your situation. You should consult with a professional where appropriate. Neither the
publisher nor author shall be liable for any loss of profit or any other commercial damages, including
but not limited to special, incidental, consequential, or other damages.

Jossey-Bass books and products are available through most bookstores. To contact Jossey-Bass directly
call our Customer Care Department within the U.S. at 800-956-7739, outside the U.S. at 317-572-3986,
or fax 317-572-4002.

Jossey-Bass also publishes its books in a variety of electronic formats. Some content that appears in
print may not be available in electronic books.

Library of Congress Cataloging-in-Publication Data

Burgess, Gloria.
    Dare to wear your soul on the outside : live your legacy now/Gloria J. Burgess ; foreword by
Angeles Arrien.
        p. cm.
Includes bibliographical references and index.
    ISBN 978-0-4702-4183-7 (pbk.)
        1. Conduct of life.   2. Soul.   3. Self-actualization (Psychology)   I. Title.
BJ1595.B78   2008
170'.44—dc22

                                                                                2008021039

Printed in the United States of America
FIRST EDITION
PB Printing   10   9   8   7   6   5   4   3   2   1

TABLE OF CONTENTS

*To my mother and father, Mildred and Earnest:
with love and gratitude for your legacies of vision,
service, and possibility.
To my husband, John, whose servant heart embodies
legacy living.
To my daughter, Quinn: may your soul remain lit with
righteous fire, and may the sweet music of your life continue
to transform the world.*

FOREWORD

Dare to Wear Your Soul on the Outside is a testament to the triumph of possibility, to the human spirit's power to reign over adversity, and to being of service to current and future generations.

Grounded in the importance of being intentional about the legacy that we live every moment of our lives, this book addresses four essential themes, each of which is necessary to making a better world: bringing forth our signature gifts, healing, transformation, and stewardship. When we pay attention to each of these themes, we will mend our own souls, our relationships, our workplaces, and our communities and thereby mend the world itself.

Drawing on her African, Native American, and Celtic cultures of origin, Gloria Burgess creates an exquisite tapestry that deftly weaves the rich threads of the past, bountiful blessings of the present, and veins of wisdom for the future. Employing her myriad gifts as a storyteller, poet, healer, and spiritual ally, her book brims with expert counsel, engaging stories, reflective questions, poetry, and affirmations that radiate joy, thanksgiving, faith, love, and hope. This book is a valuable resource and an irresistible invitation

- *To embody gratitude*—to bless the ancestors who built roads and bridges to give us a solid place to stand and to transport us beyond our differences to comprehending and embracing our shared humanity. To bless the current and future generations by planting seeds to nourish them as they grow branches of possibility, imagination, inspiration, and hope.

- *To embrace love*—to lift our voices and bring forth what has heart and meaning, not only for ourselves but for others as well. For when we express our heart's desire, we favor our soul's song over our ego's plaintive cry.
- *To embody and integrate* the Seven Sacred Promises of legacy living as a way of being, the promises of **gratitude**, **faith**, **love**, **vision**, **integrity**, **creative action**, and **legacy**. These time-honored spiritual practices are at the heart of living a contemporary life that is characterized by a long stride of spirit, a life that reengages perennial wisdoms, creativity, generativity, and deep generosity into current and future generations. These intentions and practices ultimately support positive change and transformation, which further aligns us with our inherent natures.

Gloria Burgess offers us a timely and relevant book that reminds us that our calling is to honor our spiritual inheritance by transcending the destructive narratives of pride, scarcity, injustice, conspicuous abundance, insufficiency, privilege, and inferiority. Ultimately, we have an urgent summons to rise above the weight of our personal and cultural history, to surrender whatever story we might harbor, to claim authority over our circumstances, and by doing so to transform our lives. We then offer ourselves as legacy—as radiant story, hallowed poem, glorious song, healing stream that tenders the waters of revival, healing, and transformation.

Angeles Arrien

WITH GRATITUDE

Abiding thanks to God for ordering my steps. And deep appreciation to the ancestors for their legacy of gratitude, unshakable faith, perseverance, triumph, and joy.

With joy and gratitude

- *To my dream team:* Andrea Hurst, my agent, who read my previous book, *Legacy Living*, immediately grasped it, and saw possibilities for this one. Julie Brockmeyer, who collaborates with the eyes of her soul, rendering the invisible visible with exquisite skill and beauty. Jan Seymour, my developmental editor—for her keen sensitivity, creativity, and skill in excavating and unearthing what matters. Sheryl Fullerton, my editor at Jossey-Bass, who resonated with the heart of my work and inspired me to deliver my best. Donna Cohn and Joanne Clapp Fullagar, talented editorial allies, and the production and marketing team at Jossey-Bass.
- *To my pioneering allies and colleagues:* Nancy Adler, Angeles Arrien, Geoff Bellman, Peter Block, Paul Brainerd, Toi Derricotte, Cornelius Eady, Jan Levy, Eric Liu, Carolyn Micklem, Maxine Mimms, Gifford Pinchot III, Libba Pinchot, kindred stewards of our organizations, environment, and communities, for welcoming me to your table. Courageous clients, amazing students, and other faithful supporters who edify, challenge, and lift me up: Lynn Biggs, Carol Boone, Sharon Bouscher, Gloria Campbell, Joan Dever, Tim Downie, James Edmondson, Kathryn Elliott, Mary Jane Gillespie,

Dennis Ichikawa, Margy Kotick, Dan Leahy, Diana Lilla, Melanie Lococco, Pearl Mathys, John Oleson, Ramalingam Raja, Barb Robitaille, Dr. Konji Sebati, Tim Serbin, Eva Sher, Ron Sher, Anne Stadler, Molly Swain, Evelyn Wemhoff.

- *To my sanctuary of family:* Mildred, my mother—I'm blessed and honored to be a keeper of your and Daddy's dream. Earnest, my father—thank you for welcoming the people of the world into our hearts and home and for encouraging me to dream. My sister Doris, I'm grateful for your abiding love and support. My sister Annie, thank you for your pioneering spirit and steadfast faith. My sister Debbie, I'm thankful for your tenacity, brilliance, and sustaining love. Vera, sister of the hallelujah-and-shout-for-joy soul, and Adrianna, my profound gratitude for entrusting me with your story. Quinn, through you I receive news from the future. May you continue to be blessed as a vibrant, courageous, and humble instrument of soul. John, my soul mate, husband, first listener, and reader of my many drafts. I'm ever grateful for your musical gifts—composing, orchestrating, and conducting—for their inevitable flow into the swing and sway of these pages.
- *To my sanctuaries of place:* Molokai, Hawaii, and Cortes Island, British Columbia, especially the rejuvenating, healing soul of the Hui Ho'olana and Hollyhock Retreat Centers. Whidbey Island, Washington, my close-by place of solace and retreat. Mississippi, Kenya, and South Africa, where my soul sings of all that is essential.
- *To my fellow seekers:* You who care enough about yourself and others to nourish your soul and thereby transform the soul of our world. As part of my legacy, I humbly offer this book to you.

Molokai, Hawaii   Gloria J. Burgess
May 2008

INVOCATION

Welcome! Welcome to the Blessing Table. I have been waiting just for you. This book is my heartfelt offering of hospitality, an invocation of spirit, a call to possibility.

You probably have this book in your hands because you are searching for something. Perhaps you are looking for something that you believe is muted or missing in your life, or something you once had but lost in the midst of the many demands, pressures, and competing priorities in your life. Perhaps, like so many others, you are looking for something that is already yours, something familiar that you believe is just beyond your grasp, or you simply don't know how to claim it.

In our complex, evolving global village, each of us yearns for something that is undeniably and profoundly ours, something vital, something promised. Whatever you are searching or yearning for—acknowledgment, affirmation, authenticity, personal authority, forgotten or put-aside talents, belonging, community, transition, change—you will find all these gifts here at the Blessing Table. Perhaps you will even find healing and transformation.

Similar to the Welcome Table in African and African-American cultures and the values of harmonious living that undergird Asian and many other world cultures, the Blessing Table is a symbol, a set of cultural values and norms, and a way of being and living that is infused with hospitality, love, and joy.

Here, at the Blessing Table, I trust that you will find your promise. Divinely inspired, your promise is your abiding creativity. It is your birthright and the basis for everything you are and do: talking, loving, writing, praising, meditating, exercising, praying, dancing, inventing, engineering, accounting, parenting, serving, building, innovating, singing, encouraging. Our creativity is also manifest with every breath, as we re-create ourselves emotionally, physically, and spiritually.

If you are faithful to yourself and engage with the material in this book, you will move purposefully in the direction of your promise.

WHY I WROTE THIS BOOK

I wrote this book as a wake-up call, an **urgent summons** to recognize, value, and explore your own amazing possibility and creativity. Life is precious, and in the grand song of the universe, life is short. There is much to be done. Each of us has a call on our lives. This call says, "It's time to get your act together, then take it on the road." And not just for your own sake or for your own journey. This call says, "Put on your traveling shoes so that you can live your legacy, *now*, consciously and purposefully. Put on your traveling shoes so that you can **be of use** to others. Put on your traveling shoes so that you can **wear your soul on the outside**, light the way for others, and pass it on."

I wrote this book to honor the gift given to me by my mother and father when they said, "Be all that God intended you to be—no matter what, come what may." I wrote this book to honor my other teachers who poured that same gift of encouragement into me again and again—my aunties and uncles, my sisters, and my brothers, too—the gift that is now reflected back to me by my clients, students, and readers like you.

My journey has been long; my road has not been easy. Bigotry and prejudice fortified me. Just as being treated as if I was invisible taught and sometimes withered me, the sweet rain of encouragement renewed me, the rivers of love and acceptance restored and sustained me. I wrote this book because, though my soul was shaken, bruised, and silenced, along my life's path I have learned a thing or two. And as my sister-friend and fellow poet Nikky Finney would say, "I am a woman with keys." And a woman with keys moves in a particular way. Ultimately, a woman with keys has a responsibility, an obligation to help others find theirs, help them move through their rooms, cross their thresholds, unlock their windows and doors on the journey to claim their promise.

I am a healer. My individual, organizational, and community clients, and my students come to me as a radical act of faith, entrusting themselves to me on their journey as their unknown leader. I feel blessed to be called upon as a trusted ally and steward. It is an honor and privilege to be able to help others find their inner healing power.

Dare to wear your soul on the outside is a phrase I conceived and coined many years ago. As a coach, educator, encourager, and supporter, I lead retreats and workshops for those who are in search of meaning, purpose, and direction; those who are in transition; those who yearn to connect with their passion and be true to their calling; those who are ready to say *yes* to their hopes and dreams; those who yearn to be of service to others. I help them connect their skills, talents, and gifts with their passion and calling, find wholeness and inner harmony, and bring all of their gifts forward— all with the specific intention to be of service to others, to leave the world a little bit better off than it is right now. This is what it means to **dare to wear your soul on the outside**.

Now more than ever the world needs your brilliance, your voice, your unique imagination, and your particular genius. If you want to change the world, you must first change yourself. If you want to mend and heal your personal relationships or transform your team or organization from so-so to outstanding, you must heal and transform yourself. If you want your coworkers or your organization to be different, you must first be different. To change the world, a country, an organization, a community, a relationship, begin with the smallest seed of change: begin with yourself. That is what this book is all about.

If you are ready to move from searching to finding and claiming your **personal radiance**, then I invite you to respond to the call: the call to passion and wholeness, the call to joy and fulfillment, the call to claim the magnificence and bounty of your own **true voice**. By responding *yes*, you are saying that you are ready to drop the masks, come out of hiding, and claim the **transformative power** of your own true voice.

Even if you are not yet ready, this book will support you and, I hope, inspire you to get ready in a way that honors where you are on your life path. For everyone has a place, everyone has a seat, everyone is welcome at the Blessing Table. And as your host, I am here to guide you through the thresholds and across the bridges to achieve the transformation you seek.

HOW TO USE THIS BOOK

My expectation is that you will *thoroughly* use this book. Please do not expect to pick up this book, read it, and complete it in a few hours or days. I suggest that you read and work through each chapter. If something occurs to you as you read, close the book and pay attention to whatever occurred. That is your inner compass talking to you. Listen to it. Jot down what it says to you. Get some water, take a walk. Reflect on it. Come back to the book. Respond to the questions. Do the exercises. Celebrate yourself and your accomplishments with the affirmations. In working through each chapter in this way, your goal is to make the material your own, bring it into your soul, and become one with it.

As happens with the people who attend my workshops and retreats, you will know "in your bones" when you've reached an understanding of the material and of yourself. As you move through the book, be patient and gentle with yourself. Soon you will begin to see small changes in your day-to-day life. Some changes will be immediate. Others will take more time, which means there may be additional layers to sort and work through before you can completely inhabit the fullness of your soul's calling.

Should you follow the book's **Seven Sacred Promises** (I'll describe these later) in a sequential pattern, chapter by chapter? Ideally, yes. But no one's life is ideal, and surely your life is anything but sequential and linear! Your life unfolds in circles, loops, and spirals. Through my years of teaching this material to people of all ages, from all walks of life, and from many world cultures, I have found a sequence that seems to work best for the majority of people. But you may find that moving through the pages in spirals and loops will work better for you. Go ahead, experiment. See what works best for you. As you experiment, remember to keep the arc, or structure, of the book in your mind's eye. So if you begin to feel out of sorts, you know you can always circle or loop back to the roadmap presented here.

TASKS TO PERFORM

As you follow the path of this book you will be asked to do several things. The *Questions for Reflection* will support you as you learn about key concepts and try them on for size. The *Exercises* are designed so that you can apply your newfound knowledge in concrete ways and begin to integrate it. The *Affirmations* will help you to further integrate what you are learning. They will also help you know and prove to yourself that you're getting it, that you're right where you should be.

TOOLS AND RESOURCES

As you perform these three kinds of tasks, I ask you to prepare yourself first. Use a *notebook or journal* for your notes. Find or buy one in your favorite color, or one that contains artwork you especially like, or decorate a plain one yourself. Make it your own. Since your notebook will be your constant companion, be sure that it makes you feel good. Learning should be enjoyable. Along the way, your notebook will become an invaluable resource to you, providing a record of your journey, a personal treasure chest that you can come back to again and again.

Remember that there are *no right or wrong answers*. There are *no time limits*. There are *checkpoints* in the form of tasks, however, where you can self-evaluate and prove to yourself that you are making correct and thoughtful choices. The checkpoints will be most useful to you if you are sensitive to your reactions and feelings, and honest in your responses. If you feel compelled to skip a question, plan to come back to it later. Sometimes the hardest questions are those that offer the greatest reward or insight. Only by *applying and integrating your learning* will you begin to fully comprehend and internalize the power of the **Seven Sacred Promises** and how they can transform your life.

Solitude and a place you can call your own are essential. Find somewhere to read and work that will be yours alone, even if just for the time it takes to complete an exercise or respond to a set of questions. Choose time where you will have no distractions or interruptions, where you'll be free to be yourself. Surround yourself with beauty—color, texture, sound, fragrance, light—for beauty is both a tool and resource, and it is always available to you. In the *Exercises*, when I suggest that you light a candle, do so, because it will soften your soul. It will also be a blessing as it lights the way for you and for others. If you have no candles, imagine one. Simply put your palms together as if you are holding a bird, and let your candle find its way into your world and beyond.

One of the many languages of the soul, music is also a tool and resource for you. When I write, I like to listen to chant, perhaps because the tempo and musical intervals immediately invoke the attentiveness of prayer. I also like spirituals, opera, gospel, classical, and "world music," that fusion of the universal language of music with rhythms and harmonies from diverse world cultures. One of my favorite world music pieces is called "Nelson Mandela's Welcome to the City of Glasgow," a rousing fusion of African harmonies and drumming rhythms with Scottish bagpipes and dancing rhythms.

Throughout the book, I include stories and poetry—two other languages familiar to the soul. I include a diverse spectrum to give you a good idea of how my concepts work and of their practical utility in a wide variety of settings. Most of the stories are about ordinary people, most of whom you would never know, though you probably know someone like them. There are a few stories about people whose names you will recognize. A distilled form of the story, poetry speaks to us like no other art form, revealing its layers in its own time through our layers of spirit, emotion, body, and soul.

And so I will close this Invocation with my poem about responsibility, "Song to Myself," a poem about investing in the magnificence of your own true voice, a poem about devoting yourself to wearing your soul on the outside as we repair ourselves and repair our world.

> It doesn't matter to me
> > what you do or where you work.
> I want to know
> > who you are

when the sun goes down
and if you are willing
to put everything on the line
to fulfill your soul's desire.

It doesn't matter to me
how much bread you can afford
to put on your own table.
I want to know
if you will knead and wait
and bake the bread and share
your blessings at someone else's table.
I want to know
if you can look into the eyes
of the young woman
who sleeps with fear each night
the one who dared to walk
away from the hands that pummeled her.
I want to know
if you can share her pain.

It doesn't matter to me
what neighborhood you live in
or what kind of car you drive.
I want to know
what drives you
what compels you
to follow your soul's longing.
I want to know
what pierces your heart
awakens you at night and inspires you
to devote yourself to whomever
or whatever moves you.
I want to know
how many times you've opened
your heart and extended a hand
to your homeless sister or brother.
I want to know
if you will sit in the quiet dark hours

between midnight and dawn listening
to another's heartsong.

It doesn't matter to me
how many unspeakable secrets you have.
I want to know
if you will share your secrets
to liberate your demons
so they don't devour you
or those you love.
I want to know
if you will risk looking foolish
to embrace your bliss.
I want to know
if you will grasp the sleeve
of a nameless elder stumbling on his way
and lead him in from the cold.
I want to know
if you will throw away your cloak
and show your heart if you will dare
to wear your soul on the outside.

It doesn't matter to me
how many mountains
you've climbed or will climb.
I want to know
if you've fallen down
in the valley of despair.
I want to know
if you've scarred your knees
on the stones of self-abandonment.
I want to know
how long you've been hidden in the shadows
of hypocrisy prejudice addiction abuse.
I want to know
if you will stop
to light a candle and pray with others
who will surely wander there.

It doesn't matter to me
     what you *say* you will do for others.
I want to know
     if you will act
     with courage and conviction
     if you will daily cradle the frail hand
     of your mother when she no longer
     knows your name.
I want to know
     if you will look into the hazel
     gray or ebony eyes of a stranger
     and say *yes* to affirm your sister
     your brother yourself.
I want to know
     if you will take the time to be still
     call the names and pass the cup
     to honor the ancestors
     who cleared a path
     and broke new ground
     for you and your children.

It doesn't matter to me
     that you have a past.
I want to know
     if you will celebrate your present
     if you will take a stand
     declare yourself sing *I am*
     boldly and with rejoicing
     not only to the stars at night
     but to anyone
     anywhere
     without apologies
     or regrets.

PART ONE

A Call to Wholeness

"DARE TO WEAR YOUR SOUL ON THE OUTSIDE" is my invitation to you to develop your best self and respond to your soul's calling, so that you can live your legacy, now and for the future.

Each of us leaves a legacy, whether we are aware of it or not. Daring to wear your soul on the outside is a gift of legacy, of becoming conscious, so that you can live your life with purpose and intention. It is also a gift of inner harmony that helps you to align your authentic self with your calling, so that you will be of service to others. With these gifts, you transform yourself and, therefore, leave the world a little bit better off than it is now.

In the next two chapters, I will introduce you to many new concepts that will be threaded throughout the book. As your ally and guide, I will show you how to gently incorporate these concepts so that you can manifest the new life you seek.

CHAPTER 1

The Foundation of Legacy Living: How It All Began

Make yourself useful.
MILDRED MCEWEN

MY FATHER GREW UP IN THE SMALL, racially segregated town of Oxford, Mississippi, where his mother spent each spring and fall working with dozens of other men and women planting and harvesting cotton. She often worked from sunrise until sundown. My father wished his mother didn't have to work so hard, and he often told her so. At the end of each day, my father would look into his mother's eyes and say, "Someday, I'm going to live in a house in town, a house with running water." Looking at him with tired, loving eyes, my grandmother would smile and say, "Oh, Junior, you're always dreaming."

My father would just grin. "You'll see, Mama. Someday we'll have our own house, and someday I'm going to go to college, too!" He dreamed not only of going to college, but also of designing and building a house of his very own. His dreams were also fueled by his love of reading. Although my grandparents were too poor to buy books, that never stopped my father from reading every book he could get his hands on, borrowing them from teachers, and even fishing them out of the trash. The people he read about lived in different places and led different lives from the life he and his parents knew. But how could a poor, black youth living in the South during the 1930s and 1940s be able to afford college? And even if he could, there were few opportunities for a black man to attend college, let alone become an architect.

MY FATHER'S GIFT: SEEING TO THE OTHER SIDE OF THE MOUNTAIN

My father knew that it would cost a lot of money to buy a house with running water, money that neither he nor his parents had. He figured that getting a good education would be his means to leave the poverty of the South behind. The first problem he faced was finding the money for college. Though he had few prospects of finding a job, he never let a lack of money deter him from keeping his faith and his vision of a brighter future, a time when he and his parents would enjoy the fruits of a better life.

Each day after school, my father went from house to house selling seed packets to supplement the family's meager income. What little money he earned was barely enough to buy a few books, and there was none to set aside to pay for college or to buy a house. Determined and focused despite what seemed to be an impassable mountain, he never lost sight of his goals. Even after he married and started a family, my father remained optimistic that he would someday find or hear about a job where he could earn enough money to support his wife and daughters, and still save enough to go to college.

I was only a babe in arms when my father managed to get a job as a janitor at the University of Mississippi, a job that paid a black man better than most others in town. He wasn't able to enroll in classes there, and his job didn't pay enough to make all of his dreams come true, but it put him slightly closer. He took great pride in his work; he believed that whatever the job, you should always do your best. He scrubbed the floors not once but twice, and then waxed and polished them until the white linoleum glowed. All the while, my father would talk to anyone who would listen about his dream of going to college. He never expected special treatment. He believed in devoting himself to his work—"Steady and sure; you reap what you sow; hard work pays off and has its rewards"—these were the bedrock of his values, the enduring legacy that my father's parents had passed on to him. One professor took notice and started a chain of events that would change my father's life, and that of our family, in a most amazing way.

While my father worked as a janitor, he continued to read any books he could get his hands on. One of the professors, I'll call him Professor Charles, offered to let my father use his office before and after work as a quiet place to read. As I remember this story so many years later, I can still hear my father's description: "One morning before work, I was reading when the office door opened, and in walked the dean of the university, Dr. Dean Love. He wore a hat, bow tie, tan-colored suit, and his brown shoes were polished to a shine. The man spoke slowly, 'You must be Earnest McEwen.'"

Professor Charles had told Dr. Love about my father's desire to go to college and his interest in architecture. Moved by my father's passion and determination, Dr. Love continued, "Mr. McEwen, I know just the person who can help you with your dream." He reached in his pocket and handed my father a piece of paper with a name and address on it. "Now when you go to see Mr. Faulkner, tell him I sent you." Then Dr. Love extended his hand for a hearty shake.

A VISIT THAT WOULD CHANGE OUR LIVES FOREVER

A few days later, my father walked up a long pathway to a big white house on the Rowan Oak estate, with no idea what to expect when he arrived. He had heard stories about the great writer William Faulkner, but what was he really like? He knocked on the door and waited. A dark-skinned woman in a yellow dress and white apron greeted him. "You must be Earnest McEwen. Mr. Faulkner has been expecting you. Please wait here for just a moment."

His heart pounded when William Faulkner greeted him and invited him inside. My father hesitated, for they both knew the unspoken rule—blacks were allowed to work for whites, but not to socialize with them. "No thank you, Sir," my father said.

They talked for a long time in the shade of Rowan Oak's giant old oak trees. Mr. Faulkner listened intently as my father told him, "Ever since I was a boy, I've loved books. In those books, I've learned about people and places that I may never see. My wife and I have worked hard all our lives, and we want our girls to have a better life than ours. It's my dream to go to college, and to give our children a life where they can learn and be able to do whatever they want to in this world."

Mr. Faulkner felt my father's excitement, and saw the determination in his face. "Let me ask you, Mr. McEwen, where do you intend to go to college?"

"There's a college called Alcorn about one hundred miles from here. I understand it's a wonderful school that focuses on providing a solid education for black people," my father replied.

Mr. Faulkner knew about Alcorn and that it had a good reputation. He looked my father in the eye, and right there and then he offered to become my father's benefactor. All these years of yearning and now my father was about to taste the tantalizing fruit of his dreams. After a long silence, my father shook his head slowly from side to side. "Mr. Faulkner, I want to go college more than anything in the world, but I can't accept your generous offer." He paused for a moment then continued, "I just don't see how I'd ever be able to save enough money to pay you back."

Mr. Faulkner looked surprised. With a twinkle in his eye, he said, "Why, I don't expect you to pay me back!" Then he smiled. "Mr. McEwen, the only thing I ask of you is that you pass this kindness on and let it just keep on going." Mr. Faulkner told my father that he would send payments directly to the President of Alcorn College and that he would arrange to have clothing sent for our family as well. He invited my father to stay in touch and to let him know how he was doing. My father thanked him for his generosity and assured him that not only would he "pass it on," he would also stay in touch, which he did until Mr. Faulkner's untimely death almost a decade later.

As they shook hands and said good-bye, I imagine my father's face radiant, his stride strong and sure, his whole being expectant and filled with deep gratitude. When he reached the edge of Rowan Oak, my father knelt on the cool grass beneath an old oak tree and said a prayer of thanks for his family, Professor Charles, Dr. Love, and William Faulkner. As he stood, Mr. Faulkner's kind words echoed in his ear: "Pass it on." From that day forward my father did just that, offering the blessing of Mr. Faulkner's kindness to countless others. The legacy created by my father's vision and faith and by Faulkner's generosity continues to resound within our family and throughout the world.

LEGACY LIVING:
A SPIRITUAL INHERITANCE

I am a storyteller. And I am a storyteller with the hope that my stories will lead you to a life with purpose, goals, and direction to start living your legacy now. As such, I tell my stories

- To educate
- To emphasize ideas
- To encourage creativity
- To support others in their personal and professional development
- To allow a listener or reader to be encouraged by the experiences of others
- To invite a listener or reader to value her own experiences and stories, for she holds the key to the person she is and wants to become

I often tell the story of Mr. Faulkner and my father. It is a story that honors their legacies and embodies all that we have as hopes and dreams for ourselves and to be of service to others. I also tell this story to show how it laid the foundation for my own work as a writer, teacher, coach, and leader. And though it is deeply personal, this story is ultimately a universal one in which I hope you can see a little bit of yourself, both in my father and in Mr. Faulkner.

Throughout this book, I will tell many stories and will work with you through the details of others' experiences. I hope that these stories, along with explanations and thought-provoking questions, will guide you along the path to discovering and nurturing your hopes and dreams for the present, for your future, and for the future of others.

We all want to contribute something of ourselves that is worthy of our lives here on earth, that leaves the world a little better off than the way we found it. We create this **spiritual inheritance,** this contribution, by walking a path of thoughtful choices.

Your path of thoughtful choices

legacy living

service to others

spiritual inheritance

sacred promises

signature presence

passionate intention

dare to wear your soul on the outside

your calling

In this book you are given the opportunity to experience a path that in my life I have come to call **legacy living**. Legacy living is about being fully who you are and doing what you have to do because it is the only choice that simultaneously links your present with the past and the future and that ensures a congruent life. It is about living your life to consciously create something of enduring value that will benefit both present *and* future generations. And you will come to understand that you must do so with passionate intention.

Passionate intention means being deliberate about who you are, how you show up, what you do, and in choosing your words and actions. When you live with passionate intention and act on what matters to you, these decisions shape every other choice you make, propelling you forward with purpose, drive, and an unstoppable momentum into a field of infinite possibility and allure, a field that can only be known by those who accept the **dare to wear their soul on the outside**. When you accept this dare, you are being true to your inner compass, to your authentic self, to your soul's **calling**.

To wear your soul on the outside means that you choose sovereignty over your life by saying *yes* to your own hopes and dreams and *no* to someone's agenda for your life. When you connect to your passion, you respond to your calling and are then able to bring forth and manifest your **signature presence**—your unique personal attributes and the special gifts and talents that only you can offer, that can only come through you. Empowered in this way, you can follow *your* path of legacy living.

Along this path are what I see as twin goals of legacy living— wearing your soul on the outside (when what you say and what you do are in harmony *and* aligned with your calling) and being of service to others (when your focus is other-centered, not self-centered, and it is directed toward being of service to others in the here and now and on behalf of the future). To reconcile and integrate these goals into my own life, I use what I have come to call the **Seven Sacred Promises** of legacy living. My seven tools of choice are: **gratitude**, **faith**, **love**, **vision**, **integrity**, **creative action**, and **legacy**.

The Sacred Promises in this book will support you as you make this critical choice to bring forth your signature presence, thereby transforming your life and the lives of others in your family, community, congregation, workplace, and beyond.

Each of us creates and leaves our unique legacy, whether we are aware of it or not. The greatest gift we can give to others is to be intentional about the choices we make today and every day. Because he steadfastly held on to his dreams, my father manifested his vision for a better life for his family. His choices eventually led him to Ole Miss and William Faulkner, who intentionally passed on a kindness that he could only hope would be felt by future generations.

The impact of your choices creates the footprints of your life, the legacy that you live and the one by which others will remember you. To be intentional about your legacy and to live to your fullest potential, you must ponder the following questions that will serve as the foundation for moving into a realm of intention and foresight:

- *What matters to me?*
- *What do I stand for?*
- *What do I want to create and for whom?*

And further:

- *How will I inhabit my life so that I live in harmony with my values?*
- *How can I create something of enduring value to pass on to others?*

These timeless questions, adapted from the world's great wisdom traditions, are yours. Write them down on a card or in your notebook or journal. You don't need to answer them now. In the following chapters, you will delve into these and other questions to assist you on your path to legacy living. For now, simply be aware that when you answer these questions from the deepest wellspring of your passion and desire, with clear and conscious intention, they will lead you across a threshold to step boldly into the golden life that is waiting just for you. Your answers will help you shape the rest of your life. You must be clear about your answers, because the steps you take and the choices you make will become the footprints—the legacy—that you leave for those around you and for the generations to come.

My life experience and the legacy my parents passed on to me have had a profound impact on the direction my life has taken. I wrote this book to honor my parents' gift to me, with the hope that by sharing a part of their legacy I might inspire others to live with intention, find their own story, and create their own legacy. I believe that God gave me a special gift by placing me in my particular family at a particular time in our nation's history, so that I could become a bridge-maker and an ally who assists others in navigating rough waters. These gifts allow me to be a passionate champion who sees and nurtures that special spark within others, a treasurer who encourages others to live with passionate intention and who honors and lifts up those who might find themselves unexpectedly beached along the way.

BLESSING AFTER BLESSING

So how did the kindness passed on by William Faulkner affect my father's life and so many lives beyond his? Blessed by Mr. Faulkner's windfall of generosity, the following autumn my father moved my family to Lorman, Mississippi, where he enrolled in Alcorn A&M College. As promised, Mr. Faulkner became my father's benefactor, and for the next four years paid all his college expenses so that he could pursue his dream and focus on his studies without distraction. Mr. Faulkner also arranged for Dr. Love and others to send extra money and clothing for our entire family. My father and mother were grateful for these blessings. Even so, to ease the strain of providing for a growing family, my mother worked as a cook. My father took refuge in his studies, delving into science and math, eventually earning his degree in what was then called building and construction and is today called architecture.

After my father finished college, my family left Mississippi and moved to Michigan. Faulkner had told my father that with a college degree, life would be better, but it would not necessarily come easily. My father soon discovered what Faulkner meant. In the 1950s, there were few opportunities for blacks to work as architects anywhere in the country. Disappointed but undaunted, my father turned his love of reading and learning into other arenas. By day he worked as a janitor in a hospital. By night he dove into books. Reading everything he could find about hematology—the study of the nature, function, and diseases of the blood—my father eventually taught himself enough to land a job working in the hospital's blood bank, which led to his career as a laboratory technician. Many years later, drawing on his knowledge of design and construction processes, he launched another career as an automotive engineer.

True to his word, my father always remembered his debt of gratitude to Mr. Faulkner. Always sensitive to the spoken and unspoken desires of others, my father lived his life reaching out and helping those in need. As a result of his promise to Faulkner to pass it on, my father became even more passionate about encouraging relatives, friends, neighbors, coworkers, and others to complete or continue their education.

And he never forgot Mr. Faulkner, Professor Charles, Dr. Love, or their generosity. Each man, my father included, acted in a way that was quite extraordinary for their time. My family continues to deeply appreciate and reciprocate their courage, compassion, and humanity, and we have been blessed with lifelong friendships with these men. My family has also been blessed by the warm hearth of fellowship and friendship with others throughout the world.

I have always wondered what kind of faith and vision William Faulkner must have had to wear his soul on the outside, by befriending a black man at a time in our nation's history when the code of conduct in the South virtually prohibited whites and blacks from socializing. And for my father's part of this story, it took faith, love, vision, courage, and humility to be befriended by William Faulkner. This is the type of spiritual legacy I speak about in this book.

MY PARENTS' LEGACY: PAINTING ON THE CANVAS OF ETERNITY

I learned many profound lessons from my father: To dream big and, most important, to faithfully pursue my dreams even when I have no idea of how to make them happen. Watching my father,

I witnessed the power of faith—the kind of faith that goes beyond trusting or believing, the kind of faith that is grounded in knowing that God will make a way no matter what the present circumstances look like. My father had faith in God and believed in himself. He rejoiced whenever he could "pass a kindness on" to other people.

I see my father as a visionary, an architect, a striver, a doer for the future. A tireless champion for racial equity and social justice, he was a proponent and activist for civil rights well before it became a national movement. When he and a number of other students were faced with racial discrimination and the denial of their civil rights by a faculty member and the trustees, in his role as president of Alcorn's student body my father and a handful of other students led a peaceful protest calling for the faculty member's resignation and a student body walkout. All of the students stood up for fair treatment and social justice, knowing that they were risking their hard-won education. That same day, the trustees issued an ultimatum that all students were to return to their classes or else they would shut Alcorn down. That day, the trustees also expelled my father and the other student body leaders. They were instructed to leave Alcorn's campus immediately. With the assistance of the National Association for the Advancement of Colored People (NAACP), my father finished the final three months of his undergraduate degree and graduated with honors from Central State College in Wilberforce, Ohio. My father knew that he belonged to the civil rights movement; he also knew he belonged to a God who gave him the courage to stand up for his own and others' rights and who embraced all men and women regardless of their heritage or their beliefs.

I have also learned many profound lessons from my mother. When I was a little girl, I recall my mother saying to me and my sisters, "Make yourself useful," even if we were already occupied doing something. Today her words echo in my spirit as the voice of legacy. Early on, she taught me and my sisters that you make a living by what you choose as your work or profession, and you make a life by what you do for others.

Recently, I asked my mother what compelled her to go along with my father's "impossible" dreams. She said, "I loved your father and I believed in him. More importantly, we had an abiding faith in Almighty God, for He never gave us more than we could handle, and His grace always saw us through." Even when she didn't have any idea of how our family would make it, her love and faith sustained her.

My parents left me a legacy that valued education, character, and loving, lifting up, and helping others with no strings attached. In many ways, my parents and William Faulkner painted on the canvas of eternity with their unshakable belief in the nobility of the human spirit. Their palette was imbued with the qualities of humility, faith, and moral obligation to treat every human being with dignity and respect. My father's encounter with Mr. Faulkner was a magnificent gift from God. An archetypal story of devotion and triumph, it is also a very human story that allows us to witness the boundless capacity of the human heart.

HIS SPIRIT LIVES ON

My father fulfilled his dreams of going to college and living in a house with running water. Although he created a blueprint for his very own house, he didn't live long enough to build it. After a long struggle with cancer, my father died at the age of fifty-six. But his spirit lives on through the lives of the many people he touched: family, friends, coworkers, and who knows how many others. At my father's funeral, when the minister invited the family to enter the chapel to pay our last respects, he expected just the members of my immediate family. The minister was delightfully overwhelmed when several hundred people poured into the tiny chapel—an extended family of relatives, friends, and family of the heart.

How glorious and gratifying to witness the hand of this legacy of kindness in my life and that of my entire family, all begun a few years back between two passionately intent yet ordinary men steadfast in their values:

> My oldest sister, Dr. Doris McEwen Harris, is a former school superintendent who made a point of knowing the administrators and teachers as well as engaging with students' parents, holding potlucks and town meetings, and encouraging them to be involved in the community.

She became familiar with students by visiting their classes and riding the bus and having lunch with them.

My sister Annie McEwen is a community servant and social worker. She is a compassionate listener and enchanting storyteller, and children of all ages flock to her. She especially enjoys working with children who are developmentally disabled, those who tend to be left on the margins or overlooked altogether.

My sister Dr. Deborah McEwen pours her passion for children into her pediatric practice. Formerly a computer systems engineer, she returned to college in her mid-thirties to pursue her medical degree.

My youngest sister Vera McEwen was also a computer systems engineer. She also returned to college in her mid-thirties. Vera is now a cranial-sacral therapist, teacher, and motivational speaker. She is also a passionate homeschool mom.

And I, Dr. Gloria J. McEwen Burgess, am a consultant, executive coach, educator, and poet. I am also founder and executive director of The Lift Every Voice Foundation, a nonprofit organization that provides leadership training for youth.

My mother, Mildred McEwen, continues to provide spiritual support to me, my sisters, our children, and the children of many others.

We each count among our blessings my father's and Mr. Faulkner's legacy, and whenever we can, we seize the opportunity to joyfully pass those blessings on to others.

I hope that in using this book you too

- Will be inspired and able to find your path, your calling
- Will live your life with passionate intention
- Will bring forth your signature presence to consciously and decidedly create your spiritual inheritance and intentional legacy

- Will be of service to the present and future generations
- Will experience the relevance and transformative power of the **Seven Sacred Promises**
- Will *dare to wear your soul on the outside*

> *I believe that man will not merely endure: he will*
> *prevail. He is immortal, not because he alone among*
> *creatures has an inexhaustible voice, but because*
> *he has a soul, a spirit capable of compassion and*
> *sacrifice and endurance. . . . It is [the writer's]*
> *privilege to help man endure by lifting his heart.*
> WILLIAM FAULKNER

CHAPTER 2

Your Passion and Your Calling

*Each of us, as we journey through life, has the
opportunity to find and to give his or her unique
gift. Whether this gift is quiet or small in the eyes
of the world does not matter at all—not at all.*
HELEN M. LUKE

ALMOST FIVE YEARS HAVE ELAPSED since my sister Vera sent me the
following note in response to the question "What do you want to
be doing five years from now?"

Dear Gloria,

Even though I enjoy my work as a project manager, five years
from now I don't want to be working as a systems engineer. I don't
want a two-hour commute. I want to have my own private practice
doing what I truly love—helping others discover the joy of living a
healthy, balanced lifestyle.

In five years, I want to be my true self for my daughter. She's
almost two now. When she's seven, I want to be there! I want to
show her what's possible.

Vera

When I saw her a few days ago, I showed her the note she'd
written, eagerly awaiting her response. Vera almost jumped out
of her skin with excitement. "My word! I don't even remember

saying those things about what I wanted for myself and Adrianna.
But they are absolutely what I've been striving for these past five
years." Vera glanced at the date on her note and then at me, then
began listing her accomplishments.

Almost to the day! Adrianna was two years old. Now she is seven
going on eight. I started homeschooling her a year ago today,
the same day I left my engineering job so I could start my private
practice.

Thank you, thank you for showing me this note, and thank you
for your love and support to help me claim my true calling. Even
when I didn't know how I'd make ends meet, you kept encouraging
me to stay the course, to follow my inner compass. Let me tell you,
I was walking by faith, because I had no idea how I'd find the time
to homeschool my daughter and attend to my clients. Who am
I kidding? I didn't even know how or where to find clients.

But with lots of help I figured it out.

I found a space big enough to set up a fantastic learning
environment for Adrianna and a private area for my clients. When
I asked Adrianna what she wanted to call her one-room school, she
said—the Imaginarium! And I call mine the Healing Heart.

Now all I need is a steady flow of clients. I need four clients a
day to pay my bills and pay my mortgage. I don't know where my
clients will come from, but every day I pray for new ones. When
I get a new one, I praise the Lord and write my client a thank-you
note. Some of my clients even call to thank ME for sending them a
nice note.

Adrianna and I begin each day by saying "thank you" to God.
As part of her language lessons, we also say the Lord's Prayer in
Latin and Greek, followed by bible study. When I'm with a client,
she does her homework.

Every day I know that I'm living my life with Adrianna's future
in mind. Every day I'm living my life to be of use and of service to
others. I can't thank you enough for your encouragement, love,
and support.

BEYOND THE SHADOW OF A DOUBT

Our culture would have us believe that success is defined by
wealth, power, fame, influence, prestige, and position. However,
the true measure of success is defined by only one thing: your

capacity to be your authentic self, which means bringing your whole self to your relationships and to what you do—no matter who you are with or where you are. As inexorable as the tides, you will faithfully and consistently enrich your own and others' lives by saying *yes* to your calling, and you will become successful. I would say this is God's calling, however you can also refer to it as an inner voice that calls out your deepest dreams and desires, helping you to recognize and act on them.

Our word *vocation* comes from the Latin *vocare*, meaning "to call," which is derived from *vox*, the Latin word for voice. You express your voice through the work you are called to do. Kent Nerburn writes about vocation in *Letters to My Son*. He notes that both calling and voice "touch on what work really should be. It should be something that literally calls to you, as something you want to do, and it should be something that gives voice to who you are and what you want to say to the world."

Ultimately, your work will be in tune with your intensely felt need and will feed your soul's deep hunger, thus connecting your calling to your life's passion. When your vocation and your life's passion connect, you can live your life's dream and soar to your highest potential. Frederic Buechner, author and theological scholar, describes this marvelous convergence of your calling and passion as the place where your "deep gladness and the world's deep hunger meet." You'll know this marriage of your calling and passion when, like Vera, you feel that you're in your own skin and want to jump for the sheer joy of it. You'll know you're on the right road because the road signs will be written in the language of your soul: Heart, not head. Joy, not despair. Found, not lost.

Beyond igniting your soul's joy, your work must satisfy some need in the marketplace—which is significant, if you're interested in earning a wage. When this happens, you will flourish and your work will align with the practical outcome of earning an income. Vera listened to her inner voice. She left her lucrative, secure engineering job to follow her calling, giving voice to who she really is and saying what she really wanted to say to the world. Now, as a cranial-sacral therapist, she's satisfying the needs of her clients and meeting her own and her daughter's needs. As Vera attests, a paycheck is important. You have to buy food and pay the rent. She admits, "There have been times when I've wondered, am I crazy, or what! I gave up a cushy job, a steady paycheck, employer-paid benefits, and then some!" That's when she counts her blessings and tunes in to her inner voice, which gently reminds her just how much her clients need her healing touch and how much her young daughter needs her mom's nurturing presence. During the early stages of her practice, Vera was paid less in monetary income and more in psychic income, in which the soul keeps account. Now that she's built up her client base, she is sufficiently rewarded in monetary income and many times over in spiritual income.

Because you are apt to hear diverse voices beckoning to you, each touting different kinds of work, you need a way to discern God's voice, or your inner voice, from the many other voices that vie for your attention—the voices of well-meaning friends, loved ones, peers, even your own overt voice. To help you discern, Buechner offers this rule of thumb: "The kind of work God usually calls you to is the kind of work (a) that you need to do, and (b) that the world needs to have done." If you can say *yes* to both needs, you can be reasonably sure that your work is what you have been called to do. But as Buechner cautions, if you are called to be a writer and are passionate about writing, but you're writing banal advertising copy for liquor or cigarettes, then there is a disconnect between your calling and your response. Or if you're working as a salesperson interacting with numerous people day in and day out, and you go home irritated and cranky because you'd rather be working in solitude, then your work satisfies the needs of the marketplace but not your own needs, and there will still be a disconnect between the call on your life and your response. In either case, the end result is disconnection, which manifests as discord and discontent. The antidote for disconnection is to embrace your passion by saying *yes* to your dream, to what you have been called to be and do.

A few months ago, I heard well-known political organizer and activist Donna Brazile speak about her passion and calling. One of nine children, she says she fought her first political battle at age nine when she successfully campaigned for a city council candidate who promised a playground for her poor, working-class New Orleans neighborhood. Brazile says, "What I love the most about my work then and now is 'stirring the pot' to effect change."

Though her early campaign experience gave her a sense of what she wanted to do with her life, Brazile says when Dr. Martin Luther King Jr. was assassinated, she knew beyond the shadow of a doubt what she was called to do. The next day, she dedicated her life to social justice and political activism. She recognized her passion and calling, and has responded to it ever since. As Brazile reflected on her three decades in the political arena, she talked about some of her passions: organizing demonstrations to make Dr. King's birthday a national holiday, lobbying for student financial aid, and working on or leading campaigns for former President Bill Clinton as well as for several presidential hopefuls, including Michael Dukakis, Jesse Jackson, and Al Gore. As head of Al Gore's 2000 presidential campaign, she became the first African-American woman to conduct a major political campaign.

In addition to politics, Brazile's passions also include family and cooking, New Orleans style. When someone in the audience asked how she dealt with the inevitable roadblocks in her life, she responded with characteristic, down-to-earth advice. To my ears, it sounded like a recipe for legacy living. Many of the ingredients she learned from the woman whom Brazile described as "the diva I want to become," her grandmother:

- In order to be somebody, you have to first be yourself.
- Live with love and live with joy.
- Character counts.
- Discipline matters.
- Never grow weary of doing good.
- Know where your joy comes from. Rely on it to get you through the day.
- Find your passion, something to dedicate your life to. Be driven by your purpose and your convictions.
- Keep your eyes focused on the goal. Don't get sidetracked on small stuff.
- Always be prepared to make a difference, the difference only you can make.
- Be prepared to remake the world the way you want it to be made.
- If you want change, create the wind, then you'll see the change.

- Be willing to be mentored and to be nurtured.
- Be willing to do the same for the generations coming along.
- Be a bridge builder. Be prepared to build sturdy ones for the future.
- Never give up.

MY CALL AND RESPONSE

After many years of searching, testing, and pondering, I realized I was called to build bridges in a world where there are many divides—personal, cultural, intergenerational, racial, belief system, and lifestyle. As such, I am both a bridge builder and a guide to help people get across the bridge and beyond. I use my cultural and spiritual gifts, talents, and skills to support people along their journey, inspiring them to dare to define and reach for their dreams and to have the faith and tenacity to achieve them.

Unlike Brazile, responding to my calling wasn't a direct path. In college, I was very eclectic. Because I was interested in so many subjects, I graduated with five majors. After completing my doctorate, I realized that teaching in a traditional university setting was too confining for me. Though I was passionate about my calling, the context wasn't right for me. Given my essential nature, I never dreamed I'd work in the corporate world, yet what I learned there has been invaluable in my current work. I learned a great deal about organizations—how to lead, how to successfully navigate the currents of incessant change, and how to be true to myself in spite of all. Now I'm able to live and thrive in that world and serve as a bridge for people who are subject to the ever-shifting forces of organizational life.

After thirty years, I reached the apex of my career in business. Along the journey, I learned a great deal about myself, my gifts, my passions, and the importance of responding to the calling of my heart and soul: writing, teaching, singing, theater, sharing my passions with others, and working with people to create their own legacy based on *their* passions and calling. I've found a natural connection between my temperament and working with adults and teens who are seeking, elders who want to belong yet have been relegated to the margins, baby boomers who realize that the years ahead are fewer than those already behind them, individuals who are ready to take their first tentative yet crucial steps to explore or rediscover who they really are, and organizations and community groups who are reimagining their vision and identity. Regardless of culture or context, I identify with people who feel that they don't have a voice—who are or have been oppressed, institutionally silenced, and alienated, wayfarers who have somehow taken a detour at some point along life's journey—as well as those who are looking to explore the brilliance and magnificence of their authentic voice, their essence, their passion, their soul's calling.

As I learned how to integrate my own passions into my work, again, the **Seven Sacred Promises** were my tools of choice: **gratitude**, **faith**, **love**, **vision**, **integrity**, **creative action**, and **legacy**. The following figure shows how the promises relate to one another and to your passion and calling.

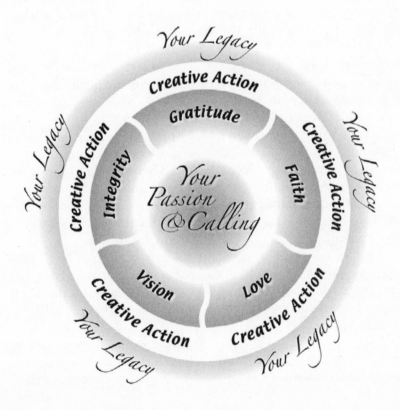

When you recognize, accept, and respond to your life's calling, you can live with passionate intention and direction. When you say *yes* to your dream and connect to your passion, then you can reach your highest potential.

YOUR PASSION AND YOUR SIGNATURE PRESENCE

When you claim, honor, and express your unique talents and gifts, you affirm your acceptance of your inheritance or legacy, or, if you will, God's inheritance or legacy for you. This is the spiritual inheritance I spoke about in Chapter One, the contribution that is worthy of your life here on earth.

Your legacy is unique to humankind, and with it comes the expectancy of choice—not just any choice but right and just choices, choices that reflect the character of greatness. When we affirm our spiritual inheritance, we are granted another precious gift, the magnificent gift of sovereignty, wherein we are the sole decision makers for our life's path. With this gift of sovereignty comes the expectancy that you will assume responsibility for your choices and actions, not just some of the time but at all times. Your responsible choices include saying *yes* to the twin goals of wearing your soul on the outside and service to others.

Living your passion can only happen if you respond to the supreme summons, the call that invites you to the union of your passion and your magnificent dream. When you do, you not only place yourself in a position to express your unique gifts and talents, what I call your **signature presence**, but you also assume sovereignty over your life, which will lead you across the threshold to the life of utter contentment and joy that is waiting just for you.

Each of us is called to become a person unique in all time. You have been summoned at this particular time to become and contribute what only you can. No one else can fulfill the legacy designed specifically for you. No one else can bring forth your signature presence.

Your expression will differ from others' because it comes through you, filtered through your values, beliefs, family history, cultural background, life experience, biases, and so on. Your expression will also differ because if you are aware, open, and receptive to others and your environment, your expression is bound to be influenced by a friend's feedback, her encouragement, curiosity, affirmation, disappointments. No matter who you are, when you are called, the summons for your **signature presence** is invariably the same: Bring forth the special gifts and talents that only you can offer, that can only come from you.

You can discover your calling by considering and thinking deeply about what you love. Not like, but love. The *Questions for Reflection* will help you. Be sure to have your notebook or journal available, and feel free to write your responses, or, if you like to draw, include your drawings as well. Your notebook or journal will be an invaluable map that charts your legacy living journey, a map created by you to help transform your life.

QUESTIONS FOR REFLECTION

Set aside time when you won't have any distractions, and remember to use your notebook or journal for your notes.

- What am I so passionate about that I would do it for free?
- If money were no object, how would I invest my time and energy?
- With whom and in what settings do I feel most comfortable, that I'm in my own skin?
- In what settings and with whom am I joyful?
- What do I love doing so much that I lose all track of time?
- When I get bored, what do I daydream about?
- What are my unique talents and skills?
- What do I do as a volunteer? What about doing this work full-time?
- What do I enjoy doing in my free time?
- If I were performing at my best and feeling comfortable expressing my signature presence, what would I be doing?
- What does the world need that I can do and that I feel joyful about?

Connecting to your passion is really about saying *yes* to your inner calling. It is saying *yes* to God's dream for you, then stepping courageously into the unknown, moving through and beyond your self-doubt, anxiety, inertia, and fear. It is saying *yes* to mystery and possibility, while letting go of your self-imposed constraints, limitations, and boundaries. The moment that you say *no* to self-imposed limits and say *yes* to yourself, you cross an invisible and very real threshold where your potential and your legacy are inextricably joined together.

If you are unsure of your calling, honor your uncertainty. Be patient with yourself. Recognizing your calling and learning to respond to it can take a long time. Your response may be a zigzag process, not a straight line. As you take your first step, test the waters and see where you end up. Move forward at a pace that's right for you. Circle around, float a while, and decide if you've truly recognized your calling. Your circling and floating may take you somewhere different than you expected. If it feels right, continue moving onward. If it doesn't, adjust and fine-tune as needed, then continue on.

When I was a young girl, I remember my father saying, "Gloria, you have a ministry." Back then, I had no idea what he meant. "Ministry," I mused, "who, me?" The only frame of reference that I had for ministry was of the person, always male, who stood behind the pulpit and preached to us every Sunday morning. In those days, I never saw a woman minister, and even if I had, I couldn't picture myself as a minister standing behind a pulpit. Now I know that my father used the term ministry to say that I had a call on my life, one that I now understand, and one that has taken years of preparation—not to mention a few zigs and zags—so that I might fully inhabit the diverse dwelling places of my calling.

I now realize that responding is a lifelong process, always in motion, always evolving. As a consultant, executive coach, educator, and parent, my ministry knows few boundaries. My pulpit presents itself within corporate, university, nonprofit, and civic settings. And that pulpit is just as likely to emerge whether I'm consulting in a boardroom with a team of executives, leading a retreat for physicians and nurses, or walking on the beach with a coaching client.

The changes you seek may be closer than you realize as you open yourself to becoming the best you can be for yourself and others. As you seek or reaffirm your calling, ask yourself these questions: What do I want to do that demonstrates who I really am? What resources or tools do I need to give my best both for myself and in serving others?

When you orient yourself to putting others first, you not only change your perspective, but you also change your behavior. Vera, whom we met at the beginning of the chapter, says it took her years to understand that service meant putting others before herself. The youngest of five children, she admits, "I thought the world revolved around me." As an adult, "I learned that it isn't about me. It's about helping others."

In her therapy practice, Vera works with military personnel who are psychologically and physically traumatized by war. She offers them her healing touch free of charge as a gift of service.

> These men and women make enormous sacrifices for us to defend our freedom. It isn't about whether I agree or disagree with war. It's about doing what I can to support them to ease their suffering and pain so they can return to a more normal life.

One Saturday each month, Vera also donates her services at a local women's shelter. Many of the women have been victims of physical abuse and are wary of anyone touching them.

> On my first day, only one woman signed up for a session with me. The next time, two women, then three. Because of their courage, others could witness the beneficial results of this non-threatening, non-invasive therapy.
>
> I've worked at the shelter for almost a year. These days, I have a waiting list. They call me "Water Woman." I'm so grateful for the courageous women who allow me to provide them with healing, therapeutic touch. Now, that's a privilege.

After years of self-absorbed, self-destructive behavior, superstar actress Angelina Jolie came to acknowledge and understand the gift of service. After reading the script for *Beyond Borders*, she recognized the parallels between her own life and that of the woman in the film—they were both women of privilege who discover that the majority of the world's population live vastly different lives. The main character in *Beyond Borders* discovers the predicament of people who are displaced due to the ravages of war and famine. As Jolie researched the film, which included months of visiting refugee camps in Cambodia, Thailand, and Tanzania, among other places, she says that something changed inside her. Not only did Jolie want to understand the plight of the refugees and orphans she met, but she realized that her astronomical income put her in a position to be of service. She could help change the refugees' circumstances, and thereby change their lives. Jolie learned how to shift the focus away from herself and focus on the needs of others. As quoted in *Reader's Digest,* she offers encouraging insights on the lessons she learned.

> You could die tomorrow, and you've done a few movies, won some awards—that doesn't mean anything. But if you've built schools or raised a child or done something to make things better for other people, then it just feels better. Life is better.

Life is so much better when your passion and calling line up. You understand the gift of your spiritual inheritance, assume responsibility for right and just choices, and you pour your signature presence into serving others. When you do, you will join Vera, Donna, Angelina, and countless others who dare to wear their soul on the outside.

> *A society in which vocation and job are separated*
> *for most people gradually creates an economy that*
> *is often devoid of spirit, one that frequently fills our*
> *pocketbooks at the cost of emptying our souls.*
> SAM KEEN

PART TWO

The Seven Sacred Promises

THE CONCEPTS IN PART ONE provided a new model for living—a model grounded in embracing your passion and calling. Doing so puts you on your path of legacy living where you can live an authentic, congruent life. To stay on this path, in Part Two I offer the resources of the **Seven Sacred Promises**: **gratitude**, **faith**, **love**, **vision**, **integrity**, **creative action**, and **legacy**. Timeless and universal, the promises will help you effectively respond to specific tasks and challenges that you will face. Each promise will unleash powerful energies to support you on your life's path.

These resources will fundamentally change how you think and behave. In these next chapters, the individual yet interdependent nature of the promises will become clearer as you continue on your path toward wholeness.

Follow your passion through the portal of the Sacred Promises. Transform your life and the lives of others as you begin living your legacy.

CHAPTER 3

What Are the Sacred Promises?

The eyes of the future are looking back at us
and they are praying for us to see beyond our own
time. They are kneeling with hands clasped that we
might act with restraint, that we might leave room
for the life that is destined to come.
TERRY TEMPEST WILLIAMS

WHAT DO YOU DO IF THERE ISN'T ENOUGH nutritious food to eat, wood for energy, or nearby sources of clean water? If your name is Wangari Maathai, you quickly connect the dots, realizing that these problems share a common origin—the steady decline of the local environment.

Educated in Africa, Germany, and the United States, Dr. Maathai was born in a village near Mount Kenya. Reflecting on her childhood there, she recalls the clear-running stream from which she and other village children fetched water for cooking, drinking, and washing.

> I would drink water straight from the stream. Playing among the arrowroot leaves I tried in vain to pick up the strands of frogs' eggs, believing they were beads. But every time I put my little fingers under them they would break. Later, I saw thousands of tadpoles: black, energetic, and wriggling through the clear water against the background of the brown earth. This is the world I inherited from my parents.

31

Today, fifty years later, all that remains of that stream is its dry bed, and the village women must walk many miles for water that may not even be clean.

In addition to the life-giving stream of her childhood, Maathai also remembers the stunning beauty of the land. And although she was still a child when they were removed, she recalls the abundant trees and wildlife that surrounded her home. Remembering the quality of life she enjoyed as a young girl, and concerned that present and future generations would never know what was lost to them, Maathai resolved to reverse the decline and restore the depleted ecosystem of her ancestral home. Not only did she want to redeem the lost wildlife habitat, but she also wanted to "give back to our children a world of beauty and wonder," a world of productivity and plenty.

Over thirty years ago, with this goal in mind, Dr. Maathai began to plant trees and encouraged others, especially the women, to do the same. She also taught them how to identify and solve habitat issues within the context of biodiversity and ecological sustainability. What began as Maathai's modest vision to restore her childhood community to its productive condition launched what is now known as the Green Belt Movement, an Africa-focused nonprofit organization that has spawned an international movement to restore devastated local ecosystems and educate citizens on ecologically sound practices.

During the past three decades, Maathai has inspired the planting of thirty million trees throughout Kenya and millions more in other countries in Africa and around the world. In 2004, when she was awarded the Nobel Peace Prize for her vision and courageous action, she was surprised: "I didn't think anyone was listening." During her acceptance speech, she acknowledged the thousands of women who caught her vision and joined her in planting trees and promoting citizen education. Hoping to inspire young people and others "to give back to the Earth that has given so much to them," Dr. Maathai said that despite the many challenges and constraints they face, she wanted them to know that there was hope and "to take inspiration from the Nobel Peace Prize."

I want to call on young people to commit themselves to activities that contribute toward achieving their long-term dreams. They have the energy and creativity to shape a sustainable future. To the young people I say, you are a gift to your communities and indeed the world. You are our hope and our future.

Dr. Maathai's work and that of the Green Belt Movement exemplifies the essential wisdom held by many indigenous peoples who remind us that "the world was not given to us by our ancestors, it was lent to us by our children." This means that our children, their children, and their children's children are primary. Their needs come first, not ours. For most of us, in our increasingly self-absorbed culture, this is a radical notion. But what if you took the indigenous perspective to heart? If someone else's future became more important than your own, how might your daily choices be different? When you answer these questions with the future *and* service to others in mind, then, like Dr. Maathai, you will have made the subtle yet significant shift in your values that is at the heart of legacy living. This shift in values will lead to a shift in your attitude, which will lead to a shift in your behavior, and this will ultimately show up in your choices and actions that define who you are and what you stand for. You will know that you have made this shift when your choices and actions are not solely focused on yourself, but on others as well.

PLANT TOMORROW'S TREES TODAY

Legacy living is about planting trees under which you may never sit, whose shade you may never enjoy. To plant such trees is to be an agent for social, cultural, political, and creative change. At this unique time in history, when our world desperately beckons for service beyond ourselves, for humanity, compassion, grace, and enchantment, each of us has an unprecedented opportunity to bring forth our signature presence. As expressed by Dr. Maathai, we have the opportunity and moral responsibility to "give back to our children a world of beauty and wonder." We are summoned to claim our calling for our own spiritual, emotional, and physical integrity, *and* to make a difference for the common good. The Sacred Promises will allow you to step into this realm of integrity with an attitude of service accompanied by creative actions that benefit the common good.

As the meaning and significance of the Sacred Promises—
gratitude, **faith**, **love**, **vision**, **integrity**, **creative action**, and
legacy—are learned, understood, practiced, and applied, you
will embark on a journey that lets you say *yes* to your calling, fully
prepared to greet the life of possibility that awaits you. Wangari
Maathai serves as an eminent example of this journey to benefit
the common good. Her inspirational journey reveals the heart
of legacy living, for this path requires a spirit of gratitude, faith,
and perseverance, hands and feet of love, a compelling vision of
a desired future, a heart of integrity, creative action, and a deep
sense of legacy, understanding that you are an instrument to pave
the way for others. Maathai recognized early on that no matter
how passionate, one person working alone can't plant thirty million trees! Because of her passionate intention, dedication, and
focused drive, she inspired and empowered others to join her
and follow her lead.

The Sacred Promises are an invitation to become a creative
ambassador on behalf of this and future generations. They provide
a path and will support you as you make this critical choice to
transform your own life and the lives of others in your "village":
your family, workplace, congregation, community, and beyond.
Each promise invites you to the wondrous union of the ground
of your being and your spiritual inheritance. Each one opens the
door to inspiration and possibility, inviting you

- To increase your awareness as you shift your focus toward the
  future and being of service to others
- To remember who you are and what is important to you
- To claim and integrate your signature presence into your daily
  life—at a personal level, in your family, work, and community
- To transcend your limiting beliefs and patterns of negativity,
  inadequacy, inferiority, insufficiency, and inertia
- To challenge your deeply held assumptions, befriend chaos,
  and welcome differences
- To become part of a community of allies who support and
  nurture each other

Each of the Sacred Promises will be discussed individually in
the next seven chapters. Each promise works in concert with all
of the other promises. Just as the individual instrumental voices

in a symphony orchestra join together to make a harmonious whole, the promises also form an interdependent composition, the impact of which far exceeds any one of the promises in isolation. By themselves or as a whole, the value of the Sacred Promises is significant. When combined with a clear sense of your calling and passion, their power increases immeasurably.

GRATITUDE

Gratitude offers the **power of blessings received and passed along**, especially in giving thanks for the blessings you receive, including the simple yet profound blessing of waking up each day to new possibilities. Gratitude requires that you acknowledge your blessings. For when you do, you can share your joy and pass your blessings on to others: your family members, coworkers, or that young girl or boy who needs you to show the way. Gratitude calls you to recognize and celebrate those who came before you, who cleared a path or built a bridge for you. When you count your blessings, share them, and express your appreciation for those who paved the way, you open your heart and allow yourself to engage more authentically with others and to the blessing waters of gratitude.

FAITH

Faith offers the **power of devotion and spiritual renewal**. One of my clients describes faith as making a commitment to think and act "as if"—until what he hopes for begins to take concrete form. Another says that faith means sowing seeds and watering them, even though you may never witness their maturation. The power of faith offers mooring in the midst of whatever storms, trials, and terrors you might encounter. On a spiritual level, faith asks you to lean in to and rely on a power beyond your own so that you might be refreshed and renewed through your reliance on grace and devotion.

LOVE

Love offers the **power of passion and heart-centered action**, allowing you to devote time and energy to whomever or whatever brings you joy. What we create with our hearts and hands is love made visible. Similarly, when you wear your soul on the outside, you embody love and radiate it to others. As Jungian psychologist Marion Woodman reminds us, when ignited by love, you burn with a fire that requires no fuel. That means that your relationships, your work, or whatever you pour yourself into feels effortless. Expressing your passion is a way of falling in love with the future, such that your actions become heart-centered instead of self-centered. Archbishop Desmond Tutu says that God treasures you and is waiting on you because He desires your help, waiting on you to acknowledge, accept, and assume sovereignty for your life. Can you imagine a more awesome opportunity? Archbishop Tutu also says that we were made for transcendence, which means that we were made to get over our own agenda and to be of service to others.

VISION

Vision offers the **power of seeing the bigger picture** and your connection to it. The Sacred Promise of vision requires you to expand beyond your normal ways of seeing, inviting you to see outwardly as well as inwardly with the eyes of your heart. When you see with the eyes of your heart, your soul responds in kind. Vision asks you to paint a picture of what you want to be or achieve and to hold on to it even when others may not be able to see what you see. If you can see your goal, you have taken the first crucial step to achieving it. Vision allows you to invest in possibility on every level—intellectually, physically, emotionally, and spiritually, creating a palpable sense of expectancy. Fueled by heart-centered action, you will inspire others to do the same by joining or enlisting their emotional and spiritual support.

INTEGRITY

Integrity offers the **power of honoring your values and wholeness**, which means knowing who you are and being true to yourself. When you stand and walk with integrity, you bring the beauty and bounty of your own true voice with you wherever you go. By fully honoring your own values and wholeness, you will be able to honor the values and wholeness of others. In this sense, the Sacred Promise of integrity affirms your kinship, shared humanity, and interconnectedness with others across generations, cultures, and other divides, compelling you to transcend differences and to honor, love, engage with, and serve others as yourself. Integrity also allows you to recognize the interrelationship of all beings and all things, and that we are part of one another, nature, and our ecosystem.

CREATIVE ACTION

Creative action offers the **power of manifestation and fulfillment**, of witnessing the concrete, tangible fruits of the Sacred Promises at work in your life. Creative action is integral to each of the Sacred Promises and also stands on its own. Creative action includes the small and big steps that are essential to move you in the direction of your dreams. The power of creative action manifests in myriad forms—through storytelling, learning, dialogue, teaching, counting our blessings, writing, loving, parenting, dreaming, painting, meditation, prayer, gardening, administration, cooking, service, dancing, planning. Creative action is the concrete demonstration of your legacy in the making, which unfolds moment by moment each and every day.

LEGACY

Legacy offers the **power of service and stewardship**, inviting you to focus on being of use to someone or something beyond yourself. Imagine yourself giving to the future in the role of provider, guardian, steward, escort, caretaker, trustee, or guide for whomever or whatever has heart and meaning for you. In this role, you will use your creativity to encourage and uplift, innovate and invent, be an architect and shape-shifter. The Sacred Promise of legacy offers you the blessing of knowing that your life counts for something, that you will leave the world a better place, using your unique signature presence to contribute what only you can. It allows you to use your calling to build on your spiritual inheritance and to pass on your blessings to others here and now and in the future, for generations to come.

SOW THE SEEDS OF INSPIRATION

As I mentioned earlier, the Sacred Promises not only support one another, but each promise is inextricably connected to all the others. Their beauty and symphonic power are fully revealed when understood and embraced as a whole. In Dr. Maathai's experience, you can see all of the Sacred Promises at work. Although I describe them sequentially, the promises always unfold in loops and spirals, just as real life does.

We see the power of **gratitude** in Maathai's appreciation for her childhood blessings of an abundant, healthy, natural environment. She gratefully embraces these received blessings. In her desire to pass them along to future generations, she steps out on **faith**: alone, Maathai began planting trees, and in 1977 she launched the Green Belt Movement, because by then her **vision** to restore a world of wonder, beauty, and healthy natural resources had blossomed into a leading conservation movement and a vast grassroots network of empowered women and men. By planting trees and teaching others about conservation, Dr. Maathai displayed a deep **love** for people, place, and habitat renewal. She brought the power of her values in restoring the **integrity** of her home-land together with her vision. All of these **creative actions** reveal an uncommon generosity of spirit and activism. Sowing seeds of compassion, Dr. Maathai's **legacy** of tree planting and improved lives continues to unfold. In addition to becoming the first African woman to win the Nobel Peace Prize, her legacy includes a litany of other significant accomplishments, including being the first black woman in eastern Africa to receive a doctorate and being elected by a landslide vote as a member of Kenya's Parliament.

As Dr. Wangari Maathai's experience shows, all of the Sacred Promises are essential for the robust, rewarding adventure of legacy living. Each of the promises demands your attention, aspiration, agreement, and commitment. Each one will bless and immeasurably improve the fabric of your life, the texture of your friendships, and the quality of your relationships at home, at work, in your community, and beyond. Like an internal compass delineating true north, the Sacred Promises will support you as you shift your focus to a vista beyond yourself, to being of service to others.

As you weave these timeless, universal promises into the fabric of your everyday life, you will find their potency fully revealed when you think of each promise as both a verb and a noun. As actions (verbs), the promises become more vibrant and meaningful as you begin to experience their power in your own and others' lives. As you commit to the promises, you will begin to internalize them, integrating your actions into who you are, into your way of being (noun).

Once you commit to acting on the promises, you will experience a paradigm shift that will transform not just your life but your entire world. Once you decide what matters to you, you place yourself in a position to make something happen. And once you set your sights on a meaningful cause or someone else's future rather than on your own, that paradigm-shifting decision will shape every other choice you make. It will propel you forward with unparalleled purpose and momentum.

Reading about the Sacred Promises and understanding their significance is just the beginning. To fully grasp their transformative power and blessing, you must make a most important promise: to experience the Sacred Promises for yourself. In the remaining chapters, you will be able to do just that. As you read the next seven chapters in Part Two, you will learn more about each of the promises through a variety of tools: stories, examples, reflective questions, exercises, and affirmations. These interactive tools will assist you in gaining a better understanding of each promise and experience its power. The last five chapters in Part Three will build on what you learn in Parts One and Two as you integrate your newly learned spiritual model in your daily life.

When you commit to experiencing the Sacred Promises for yourself, you can truly experience the life-changing power and joy of legacy living. The Sacred Promises will help you:

- Understand the significance of your vocation, your unique calling, and how you want to use your distinctive voice as an instrument for change.
- Move beyond the barriers that keep you from realizing your calling, and transport you into the bountiful life that is waiting just for you.
- Understand the significance of expressing gratitude and the power of recognizing and passing your blessings on to others.
- Move past fear and step out in faith to courageously claim your own life of fierce possibility.
- Fall in love with the future, and connect with your calling and passion so that you can be all you can be and a radiant beacon of hope for others.
- Realize your vision with boldness, confidence, and humility— all of which are essential in order to be a beacon who lights the way for others.
- Claim your authentic voice, so that you can redeem your own life and in so doing redeem the lives of others, and allow the power of integrity to propel you toward wholeness.
- Embrace your creativity in all its glorious facets as you make positive, life-affirming choices to embrace and integrate the Sacred Promises into your lifestyle.
- Move toward your dreams every single day, giving your dreams sturdy legs as you manifest your legacy.

- Stay on the path of legacy living not merely for your own sake as you live your life today, but also for the sake of sowing seeds of hope and inspiration for tomorrow.

> *Do all the good you can*
> *by all the means you can,*
> *in all the ways you can,*
> *in all the places you can,*
> *at all the times you can,*
> *to all the people you can,*
> *as long as ever you can.*
> JOHN WESLEY

CHAPTER 4

Gratitude—Blessings Received and Passed Along

*Gratitude is the grandparent and highest of
all the virtues.*
CICERO

EVERY SATURDAY, SHEILA DRIVES ONE HUNDRED MILES round-trip to visit her friend Hank. Born and raised in Montana, Hank now lives in Washington in an assisted-living home in a beautiful setting surrounded by old-growth forests and a view of a pristine lake against a backdrop of snow-capped mountains. Sheila looks forward to the drive. Leaving the hard-edged city behind and transitioning to the restive contours of the land gives her a sense of peace and tranquility. She especially cherishes the last few miles where the road is cradled on both sides by enduring stands of sequoia and red cedar. Each week as Sheila drives through this verdant cathedral, she gives thanks for her friend Hank, his family, the forest, and all the creatures in it.

> In some ways, Hank is like a father to me. I lost my dad in a car crash when I was eleven. One of my fondest memories of dad is him singing me awake. I hated to get out of bed, especially on school days. Every morning while mom prepared breakfast, dad would gently sing me awake.

Another is hiking. Every Saturday he'd take me and my three brothers into the hills to his favorite spot, and we'd hike until late morning, eat lunch on the trail then head back down. Before supper, we all helped dad wash our old pink 1960 station wagon. In the evening, we played board games or shared our funniest stories, laughing until tears rolled down our cheeks.

Hank doesn't seem to remember things the way he used to. His care-givers at the home tell Sheila that he's experiencing the early stages of Alzheimer's disease. They say that more and more Hank doesn't seem to make contact with those around him, although he still recognizes Sheila, welcoming her immediately as she enters the room.

I treasure the time I spend with Hank. I love the way he rubs his delicately-boned hands together just before he starts one of his stories. Each time he begins, his eyes light up with astonishment as though he is telling the story for the very first time. And each time he begins, I feel so grateful that I can join Hank as his "dance partner" at this stage of his life.

These days, it takes Hank almost the entire morning to wash, clothe, and feed himself, yet he enjoys the deep satisfaction and joy of being able to do these things on his own. He counts it as a blessing. I feel honored to be able to accompany him in this wondrous waltz as he celebrates the simple joys of living. I cherish the time I have with him and feel blessed to serve as both witness and accomplice in these sacred moments of the soul.

Gratitude is one of the most powerful ways to express our caring and compassion for one another and to acknowledge the blessings of our lives, as demonstrated in the enduring relationship between Sheila and Hank. It is the act of one heart greeting another, each on its own terms. Among her many blessings, Sheila counts Hank's openness to her nurturing and loving support, allowing Sheila to dance with him in the fullness of her signature presence.

Gratitude, both an emotion and a state of being, means "the quality or feeling of being grateful or thankful." Its Latin heritage, *gratus,* reveals gratitude as kindred to grateful, which includes the qualities of appreciation and thankfulness as well as the more obscure, though significant, meaning: "Pleasing to the mind and senses." Being grateful includes your ability to express appreciation and give thanks. It also includes your ability to embody a disposition of gratitude. Intimately connected to the tenor of our emotional *and* spiritual life, our expression and disposition of gratitude reflect the condition of our soul.

In her book *The Second Half of Life*, Angeles Arrien describes the many benefits of the practice of expressing gratitude. Cultivating gratitude dissolves negative feelings, such as anger, envy, pride, fear, and defensiveness. Expressing gratitude "keeps our hearts open to each other." She rightly points out that the practice of gratitude also "keeps us learning and growing, and frees our generosity." Indeed, a closed heart and being thankful will never coexist.

Though some individuals seem to be predisposed to feel grateful more often than others, everyone can experience, express, and embody gratitude. Social psychologists and mind-body researchers tell us that those who experience, express, and embody gratitude more frequently than others tend to be happier, healthier, more forgiving, more helpful, less stressed, and less depressed than those who are less grateful. In other words, gratitude is good for you. According to Blair and Rita Justice and other experts, when you express and embody gratitude, your body's chemistry actually changes, increasing the production of dopamine and serotonin, the so-called feel-good and happiness hormones. From a neurobiological perspective, gratitude is in the same sphere as the social emotions of awe, wonder, elevation, and pride.

THE BLESSINGS OF GRATITUDE

To fully experience the blessings of gratitude, you must be open to its language, to the constellation of its expression, which includes receptivity, vulnerability, kindness, acknowledgment, appreciation, thanksgiving, reciprocity, deliverance, blessing, and joy. Gratitude invites you to revel in the miraculous blessing of waking up each day to new opportunities, new possibilities, and new vistas, and to rejoice in the sacred, particularly in the sacred grace of your blessings that are unearned.

The Sacred Promise of gratitude is the inward and outward acknowledgment and proclamation of your blessings. Gratitude entreats you to give thanks for the blessings you receive. By expressing your acknowledgment, appreciation, reverence, and joy, you pass your blessings on to others, thus bringing forth the possibility of new life by sparking the spirit of gratitude in others. Each time you count your blessings, you open your heart to possibility, allowing you to tap into the wellspring of your creativity.

QUESTIONS FOR REFLECTION

Set aside time when you won't have any distractions, and remember to use your notebook or journal for your notes.

- What does gratitude mean to you?
- What is the rhythm, or presence, of gratitude in your life?
- What would it be like to take a few minutes at the end of each day to pause and reflect on your experiences and count your blessings? To jot them down on a notepad or in a journal? To thank your spouse and your children for the blessings they provide in your life? To write yourself a reminder to thank your coworker or boss for their kindness, friendship, hospitality, or word of encouragement? To give thanks to God for providing these blessings?

We express gratitude when we are receptive to and acknowledge others, see the inherent good in others, experience and revere our deep kinship with the natural world, and embrace thankfulness as a way of being. Let John F. Kennedy's inspirational words encourage you as you develop a lifestyle of gratitude: "As we express our gratitude, we must never forget that the highest appreciation is not to utter words, but to live by them."

When we express gratitude, we must acknowledge that which delights as well as that which disappoints; it is not for us to judge the lessons of our life experience. Both bear valuable fruit. When you bless both the good and the bad, this offers you the opportunity to embrace all aspects of your life.

In our fast-paced lifestyles, it is easy to devour activity and experience without taking time to slow down, digest, and reflect on their inherent blessings. To my clients who find it difficult to reflect on their blessings, I suggest that they recall just one moment, one encounter, one experience each day for which to give thanks. I also suggest that they write their reflections in a gratitude notebook or journal. More often than not, they recall not just one encounter or person for whom they are grateful, but many. Unless you slow down, reflect, and make a note of your blessings, you become like the proverbial gadabout flitting from one experience to the next without contemplating, metabolizing, or integrating the richness and fullness of the blessings inherent in daily living. Slowing down is an enormous act of graciousness, courtesy, and intention, a worthwhile step on the path to legacy living.

You can express your gratitude in countless ways. As you cultivate your own practice of gratitude, you can also be intentional about nurturing a spirit of gratitude in others. Practicing gratitude or any other promise cultivates the soul's memory and is also a practice of wearing your soul on the outside. Here are some simple ways to be what I call a gratitude champion:

- Count your blessings as you brush your teeth, prepare breakfast, or while you exercise or walk your dog.
- When you tell someone *thank you,* look into his or her eyes and say it with your eyes, heart, voice, hands—your entire body and soul. Express gratitude with your entire presence. Be as specific as you can. Though people may not recall exactly what you say, they will remember the warm feelings that accompany your thank-you.
- Call a friend who has been a blessing in your life, and with a smile in your heart and voice, thank him or her. Follow up by sending your friend a personal, handwritten note. Include a tea bag, a packet of seeds, or a few postage stamps.
- Help children learn the language of gratitude through words, pictures, stories, poems, games, puppetry, and songs.
- If you don't have children or your children no longer live with you, volunteer to work with children in your local school, church, or community center. Teach them about the importance of gratitude in their daily lives.
- Teach children the connection between gratitude and chores, helping them appreciate their blessings and recognize the intrinsic value of a task well done.

- Set aside time to help children write thank-you cards and notes to relatives and friends. Encourage them to send thank-you cards and notes that are not related to birthdays or other special occasions but rather a note of "just because" appreciation. This also teaches the importance of being grateful to and for others. Very young children can create simple cards using construction paper, markers, crayons, stickers, and rubber stamps.

RECONSTITUTE YOUR SOUL

When we create the spaciousness in our life to attend to, honor, and give thanks for the blessings that are all around us, we provide the necessary nourishment to feed and reconstitute our soul. Then miracles abound. We recognize the miracle of breath. The miracle of rain. The miracle of a child's laughter. The miracle of grass frost-slick beneath your feet punctuated by the occasional crunch of autumn leaves. The miracle of a mare's breath, its warming vapor rising as she stands watch at the edge of a dusk-blue field.

Miracles are as close as our attentiveness will allow.

The world's faith, wisdom, and artistic traditions espouse this truth, eloquently captured by Franz Kafka: "You do not need to leave your room. Remain sitting at your table and listen. Simply wait. Be quiet, still, and solitary. The world will freely offer itself to you to be unmasked. It has no choice. It will roll in ecstasy at your feet."

Those precious moments of spaciousness may be fleeting; you must be attentive to them and seize the moment to express your gratitude.

> Late one spring afternoon after a long spell of overcast Seattle
> weather, the sun briefly breaks through the leaden clouds, and
> I behold the miracle of an unexpected gold and persimmon sunset.
> In that moment when the sun appears, my daughter steps into
> the room, and I am blessed to bask in the sun's warmth and her
> luminous presence. As she presses her small face against mine,
> I tell her what a precious blessing she is to me and her father.

After eleven years of marriage, my husband's and my desire for a child was surpassed only by our frustration at not being able to conceive. Imagine our delight when, at thirty-three years old, I discovered that I was pregnant. We were positively elated. Just a few weeks before I became pregnant, I had enrolled in a weight loss program. When I told the physician that I planned to take a hiatus from the program because of my pregnancy, he recommended that I stay in the program. But to do so, he nonchalantly informed me, I would have to have an abortion. Astounded and horrified, I dismissed the doctor's advice.

Because I was born into a large extended family, I naturally expected that my husband and I would be blessed with several children. God had other plans for our lives. For one brief moment, He opened the door to usher in a new life. After Quinn was born, that door closed. My husband and I continue to thank God for blessing us with our miracle pregnancy, our miracle child.

When I'm alert to the miracles that are all around me, I join E. E. Cummings in his ecstatic psalm that celebrates the sensual, ineffable miracle of creation, and I can't help but rejoice:

> i thank You God for most this amazing
> day:for the leaping greenly spirits of trees
> and a blue true dream of sky;and for everything
> which is natural which is infinite which is yes

> (i who have died am alive again today,
> and this is the sun's birthday;this is the birth
> day of life and love and wings:and of the gay
> great happening illimitably earth)

> how should tasting touching hearing seeing
> breathing any—lifted from the no
> of all nothing—human merely being
> doubt unimaginable You?

> (now the ears of my ears awake and
> now the eyes of my eyes are opened)

Who knows what blessings are in store for you? Who knows in what kind of package your miracles will arrive? When they do, how will you recognize and acknowledge your blessings and pass them on to others?

AFFIRMATIONS: I'M DOING IT!

- I routinely count my blessings.
- I let others know that I am grateful.
- I keep a gratitude journal.
- I know that when I offer blessings to others, I am blessed in return.
- I regularly send thank-you notes or call others to say thank you.
- I bless both my positive and painful experiences and circumstances.
- I look others in the eye when I say thank you.
- I am committed to helping others grow by expressing gratitude.
- I am aware that gratitude creates positive effects—emotionally, physically, and spiritually.

EXPRESSIONS OF GRATITUDE

Prayer, ritual, and ceremony are time-honored ways of expressing gratitude. Most of us learned prayer at a very early age when we began to say grace before meals. In the community in which I grew up, everyone I knew recited some version of this prayer before each meal:

> God is great, God is good.
> Let us thank Him for our food.
> Bow our heads, we must be fed:
> Give us, Lord, our daily bread.

My Caribbean cousins call this kind of prayer "turning thanks." As a child, each night I knelt beside my bed, bowed my head, and into my clasped hands I prayed for my family, friends, and for the keeping and tending of my soul while I slept. Though I no longer begin with the words of my childhood prayer, "Now I lay me down to sleep," I continue this practice of nightly prayer.

As with prayer, ritual and ceremony also invite the sacred into our lives and open the door to blessings. Ritual and ceremony allow us to step out of ordinary time, where we often feel rushed and in constant motion, and cross the threshold into a time out of time known as *kairos*, or sacred time. The rhythm of *kairos* is governed by a slower, less hectic pace, the rhythm of the eternal.

Rituals should renew and restore you. Before taking a soothing soak after a long work day, you can enjoy the ritual of lighting candles to give thanks to those who light the way for others, and you can burn incense to give thanks for the joy of being alive. As part of her morning ritual, one of my clients enjoys a bowl of steamed rice: "My father worked most of his life as a rice farmer. I savor the aroma and taste of the rice on my tongue. As I consume it, I whisper blessing words to my father, thanking him for spending so many long days and years in the fields to feed and support his family. He passed away long ago. My morning rice ritual helps me feel connected to him."

In my poetry performances, I always begin with a poem of gratitude to honor my poetic and biological ancestors. This ritual is a way of gentling myself and inviting the audience into a small glimpse of my world.

Ceremony can transport you from the commonplace and elevate you into the extraordinary. It invites reflection and replenishment, and ushers in nourishment for your soul. Ceremony also provides you with the fullness of time to recognize and honor what is important and significant in your life. Cultures around the world use ceremony to celebrate and pay tribute to occasions, events, places, and people who have special meaning: births and birthdays, adoptions, naming, puberty, graduations, marriages, menopause, divorce, a new home or office, travel, christening ships, our earth, retirement, and death.

Before you consider the next set of *Questions for Reflection*, light a candle and imagine a vase filled with your favorite flowers. Breathe in their fragrance and let the eyes of your heart appreciate their color.

QUESTIONS FOR REFLECTION

Set aside time when you won't have any distractions, and remember to use your notebook or journal for your notes.

- In what ways do you express gratitude through prayer, ritual, or ceremony? Is it daily or occasional?
- Do you recall any seasonal or annual rituals or traditions from your childhood? If so, what special qualities do you remember—such as food, sounds, smells, colors, textures, people, locations, time of the year?
- Have you created or adapted any traditions or other routine activities into your life? For example, each Thanksgiving, rather than cooking a big family meal, my neighbors and their teenage sons serve food at the local mission.
- Have you created any prayers, rituals, or ceremonies to celebrate special occasions or events in your life?
- Have you created any prayers, rituals, or ceremonies to honor a significant person or event in your life? What special qualities did you celebrate?

I recently attended a conference during which an entire session was devoted to ritual and ceremony. The session was a tribute to Dr. Asa Hilliard, one of the scheduled speakers. Due to his unexpected death only a few months prior to the conference, the planners used the session to honor his legacy as historian, educator, and pan-African scholar. Aligned with the Sacred Promise of gratitude, the festive, respectful ceremony included a moving invocation and retrospective of Dr. Hilliard's life. The ceremony also included the ritual of "calling the ancestors," a ritual that paid homage and appreciation to the women and men on whose shoulders Dr. Hilliard stood and who paved the way for us all.

There are many ways to express gratitude to those who have paved the way for us. My friend and colleague Nancy Adler has taught and consulted on global leadership and management for many years. In the past decade, she has devoted herself to developing her own artistry as a painter and reimagining the purpose and function of art and artistry in developing leaders and in the practice of leadership.

A few years ago, Nancy sent me an article she'd written, "Speak Your Truth," in which she discusses the importance of tending to your creativity—in whatever form it takes. Recognizing that birth is one of the ultimate forms of creativity, Nancy acknowledges her ancestors by expressing her profound gratitude and love to her great-grandmothers for her own birth and life in this letter of remembrance.

Dearest Laura and Nina,

How do I thank you for your ultimate sacrifice? From the stories my mother told me, I know that in the ultimate act of courage and love you demanded that your children (my grandparents) escape the Nazis and leave their home city of Vienna, even though it meant leaving you behind. My mother told me how you pleaded with your children to board the train with the four precious tickets and hard-gotten passports. You begged them to escape so the family might live, so that I might be born.

On February 5, 1939, the train pulled out of Vienna bound for Switzerland, with your married son and daughter and their two children, including Liselotte, my then 14-year-old mother-to-be, aboard. The clandestine escape led the family circuitously from Austria through Zurich, London, New York, and then ultimately on to California.

Dearest Laura and Nina, how do I wear this precious cloak of life that you so valiantly bequeathed to me? I can't erase history, the fact that you were murdered in the concentration camps in Treblinka and Auschwitz, but hopefully in the day-to-day reality of my safe and privileged North American life, I have found a way to honor your names.

Hopefully, with your love and courage supporting me, through my teaching, writing, and painting, I can be one more voice connecting us through our profound humanity across the divides of culture, language, religion, ethnicity, and nationality that have tried so hard to extinguish our ability to live peacefully together and share the planet.

With profound love,
Nance
Your great-granddaughter

Many years after the Nazis murdered her great-grandmothers, Nancy wrote this letter to Laura and Nina to express her gratitude, assuring them that through her life and work their legacy of love and courage lives on. As a professor of international leadership and management, Nancy encourages and challenges managers and peers to find and draw inspiration from their sources of gratitude just as she has found hers in the bountiful cloak of life passed on to her by her great-grandmothers.

As you prepare to complete the next set of *Exercises*, ask yourself, "Who has blessed me by paving the way for me?"

EXERCISES

Set aside time when you won't have any distractions, and remember to use your notebook or journal for your notes.

- Jot down the names of three relatives or other loved ones whom you would like to thank for being in your life. For each person on your list, jot down what you're most grateful for. Write each person a thank-you note. You can send the notes or keep them for yourself.
- Find some memorable photos of your favorite relative or another loved one and tape or glue it in your notebook or journal. Write a note about why this person is your favorite.
- Scan your photos of your favorite relative or another loved one and create a slide show or video. Include his or her favorite sayings. Add quotes, poems, and music.

LOOK IN THE MIRROR

When my daughter was a toddler, whenever I was about to leave for a business trip out of town, she'd grab me around my legs and plead with me not to go. Her pleading tugged at my heart. Her insistence on my presence was a wake-up call that forced me to look in the mirror and come to terms with my expressed values and my daily choices. My walk was out of step with my talk. My talk said, "Family is important." At that time, however, my walk said something entirely different to my daughter.

To spend more quality time with her, I eventually left my work in the corporate world and launched my own consulting practice, which gave me greater flexibility in my work schedule and more time to spend with my daughter. This gift of spiritual chiropractic also allowed me to be more conscientious about how I expressed my signature presence at home and at work.

Not only did my daughter's tug on my heartstrings help me focus my time and energy differently, her insistence on more of my presence in her life compelled me to answer the questions that I asked in Chapter Two in an entirely new light:

- *Who am I?* I am Quinn's mom. I am the only mother she has or will have. At this stage in her life, my work is to serve her. Not my profession, my career, or my employer.
- *What do I care about?* I care about my work and being of service to others. I also care about Quinn. I care about her present and future more than anything, including my work. Mothering Quinn is my service to others, my legacy in the making.
- *Who and what matter?* My daughter matters. I am a steward for her, so I must look in the mirror and, if needed, rearrange my priorities, for the choices I make each moment of each day are the legacy I weave and the one that I will leave behind. My legacy to Quinn is the story by which she knows and relates to me here and now and by which she will remember me and my impact on her life.

I'm deeply grateful to her for reminding me that before I care for others, I must practice what I preach, align my walk with my talk. I must first take care of matters in my own home—literally and figuratively—so that I might walk and serve with passionate intention and integrity at home and beyond.

Gratitude unlocks the fullness of life. It turns what we have into enough, and more. It turns denial into acceptance, chaos into order, confusion into

clarity. . . . It turns problems into gifts, failures into
success, the unexpected into perfect timing, and
mistakes into important events. Gratitude makes
sense of our past, brings peace for today and creates
a vision for tomorrow.
MELODIE BEATTIE

CHAPTER 5

Faith—Devotion and Spiritual Renewal

Faith is the first factor in a life devoted to service.
Without faith, nothing is possible. With it, nothing
is impossible.
MARY MCLEOD BETHUNE

AFTER LEARNING OF THEIR YOUNG SON'S impending blindness
due to hereditary glaucoma, the parents of Italian tenor Andrea
Bocelli were determined to raise him to live a normal life. In her
biography of Bocelli, Antonia Felix writes that his mother and
father were adamant that they "wanted to make a man, not a
handicapped person."

When Andrea was old enough to begin elementary school, his
parents searched throughout Italy until they found a school whose
approach was in concert with their beliefs about raising a blind child.
In school, he learned to read Braille and to play soccer and other
team sports. Thanks to his grandfather, Andrea also learned to ride
horses, a passion he has sustained into his adult life.

Though he recognized his passion for singing at an early age,
as a young man Bocelli sidestepped his musical calling to pursue a
more practical profession as a public defender. However, it wasn't
long before he made the life-changing decision to leave the security
of civil service behind. After working as a public defender for a

year, Bocelli stepped out on faith to follow his musical calling. For Andrea it was a matter of yielding to his "sense of responsibility to develop the God-given talents that gave him and so many others pleasure."

Through the years, Bocelli has worked fiercely to achieve his dream of offering songs from the heart. The love and rigor demonstrated by his parents "to make a man, not a handicapped person" and the lessons that Andrea learned as a young boy about blindness, sports, horses, music, and faith in himself manifested as his "refusal to accept defeat." Today, a celebrated singer of both classical and popular music, Bocelli performs for sold-out audiences all over the world.

BELIEVING IS SEEING

The Sacred Promise of faith allows you to say to yourself, your spouse, coworkers, friends, family members, "I trust myself. I can do it." When your circumstances seem unclear or uncertain, faith invites you to understand that *believing* is seeing: your belief provides the faith to construct the bridge that supports you as you respond to your calling and claim your life's purpose. Bocelli's faith became a bridge as he left his secure post as a public defender. Walking by faith, he crossed the bridge to fulfill his calling as a professional musician. This same faith carried Bocelli as he was transported from being a virtually unknown, yet gifted, tenor to a world-renowned performer.

In *The Creative Spirit,* Daniel Goleman and his coauthors, Paul Kaufman and Michael Ray, identify faith as one of four resources, or tools, that you can access to develop or enhance your creativity. These tools are "faith in your own creativity, absence of judgment, precise observation, and penetrating questions." The authors attest that faith in your own creativity and absence of judgment—which also demands a posture of faithfulness—is the knowledge "that you have a power within you that is always available to you." And, I would add, the more you tap into it, the more that faith increases.

In our common vernacular, we talk about steps, walks, leaps, and even flights of faith. The latter suggests that faith is something elusive and ephemeral rather than concrete and tangible; faith, however, contains all of these elements. In his letter to the Hebrews, Saint Paul writes that faith is "the *substance* of things hoped for, the *evidence* of things not seen." In other words, faith is being *sure* of what we hope for and *certain* of what we do not see. I've italicized key words to emphasize these essential aspects of faith.

Author and theologian Andrew Murray describes faith as a sense not unlike our other senses of sight, hearing, touch, taste, and smell. "Just as we have our [five] senses, through which we hold communication with the physical universe, so faith is the spiritual sense or organ through which the soul comes into contact with and is affected by the spiritual world." Through this spiritual sense, this organ called faith, you can communicate with a force outside of yourself. In your communion with that force, you can know that something hoped-for will manifest, that something you do not see will indeed become real, concrete, tangible. In the ancient Greek sense of knowing, you can be confident—full of faith—because your soul has experienced contact with the spiritual realm, with a force outside of and greater than yourself. Faith is ultimately a direct, though inexplicable experience. For if someone were to ask you to "explain" or "prove" such an experience, you would not be able to do so. Yet you would stand firm in your belief that something happened as a result of your having faith.

The fabric of faith includes belief, trust, confidence, and hope, as well as surrender, fear, and doubt. This means that your step, walk, or great leap of faith may not necessarily proceed in a straight line. Like any other aspect of creativity, the Sacred Promise of faith invites you on an exhilarating adventure to unearth the treasure of your soul. For Andrea Bocelli, his faith in himself resulted in a brilliant career that now affords him the personal reward of wearing his soul on the outside, and rewards the world with his rapturous, celestial voice, the unearthed treasure of his soul.

FAITH IN ACTION

The Sacred Promise of faith allows you to reach out with confidence to fulfill your soul's desire. You were created to act on faith. By doing so, you say *yes* to the paradoxical requests of belief and doubt, hope and fear. You also demonstrate your devotion to your calling, your values, your belief in the awesome beauty of your own true voice. In *Writing and the Spiritual Life,* Patrice Vecchione describes your voice as essential to you and others. Your voice is "your own natural resource. Its worth in your life and in the lives of others may match the birds' need for sky."

The prized resource of your voice yearns for the fire of faith to keep it lit and vibrant. The Sacred Promise of faith invites you to tend the fire of your voice at a four-sided hearth, each with a specific name and purpose: **faith in yourself**, **faith in your own calling**, **faith beyond your calling**, and **faith beyond yourself**. Most of us tend to prefer one side of the hearth most of the time. But to experience the fullness and brilliance of your own true voice, you must tend to the fire from all four sides every day, if only to sweep away the ashes. In this way, each fire of your faith will stay lit, keeping you more deeply connected to yourself, to your calling, and to others.

Faith in Yourself

A monumental gift, faith in yourself empowers you to respond to your calling, fulfill your vocation to the best of your ability, and bring forth your signature presence and the resonance of your own true voice. Faith in yourself supports you as you triumph over the would-be saboteurs of self-doubt, caution, and voices of negativity, insufficiency, inferiority, and inadequacy. At this hearth of faith, you will hear the sound of your own voice saying, "Go for it! You can do it." You will also hear your voice say four of the most important words that anyone can say to herself or another person: "I believe in you." This hearth of faith holds the key that will unlock the door and liberate you from your self-imposed prison, allowing you to lift off and soar on the thermals of your God-given gifts.

During a recent coaching session, my client Ana confided:

> I struggle to think about faith in myself. Faith and faith in me don't seem to align in my thoughts. Though I jerk at the thought of having faith in myself, last Friday as I sat in the Kansas City airport knowing I had to create a presentation for the Project Management Institute on Monday evening, and I just didn't have energy to think about it. . . . I heard a little voice inside me saying, "Have faith in

yourself, you'll get it done." I don't know if that was procrastination or what, but I found myself trying on faith in me in that small way.

By simply trusting her inner voice, Ana took the first important step of faith. If the idea of having faith in yourself seems a bit daunting, follow Ana's lead. Begin with a small step. Sit by the hearth and try on faith in yourself. Each time you take a step of faith, the next step becomes easier because you've done it before.

It is important to recognize that when you believe in someone or something, your faith will be tested. This is a given. When your faith is tested, you may be inclined to surrender your belief in your project or new idea. Don't give in or give up. Each time that you are tested and you don't change your mind, your faith will grow stronger, and you will become more resolute.

As you prepare to complete the next set of *Questions for Reflection,* consider faith as it relates to other aspects of the natural world. For example, when the willow tree is tossed by wind and rain, it visibly bends until its branches kiss the ground. Beneath the ground, unseen by us, its roots grow deeper. The more the wind bends the tree, the bigger, stronger, and deeper the roots grow. And when your faith is tested by the inevitable challenges that you will face, take heart. Like the willow tree, your faith will grow, strengthen, and deepen.

QUESTIONS FOR REFLECTION

Set aside time when you won't have any distractions, and remember to use your notebook or journal for your notes.

- What does faith in yourself mean to you?
- What is the rhythm, or presence, of faith in your life?
- List an activity that you enjoy, such as running, swimming, dancing, or rock-climbing. To learn this activity, what acts of faith were required of you?
- In what ways—small or big—have you trusted yourself or said, "*I believe in myself*"?

Faith in Your Own Calling

Whether or not your calling involves work or earning a wage, faith in your own calling is essential because only you can respond to the calling designed for you, and your calling can come only through you. At this hearth of faith, you will experience the fire of your unswerving fidelity to your uniqueness. You will hear the sound of your own voice boldly declaring, "This is who I am. Look out world, here I come!"

Modern dance pioneer Martha Graham reminds us not to dampen or block our uniqueness, our signature presence. She tells us that if you do, "It will be lost. The world will not have it." Moreover, she says, "It is not your business to determine how good it is; not how valuable it is; not how it compares with other expressions. It is your business to keep it yours clearly and directly. To keep the channel open." If you suppress or hide your signature presence, you miss out and so do others. So does the world. Let your light shine through you and light the way for others.

EXERCISES

Set aside time when you won't have any distractions, and remember to use your notebook or journal for your notes.

- Create or find a quote that captures the essence of what faith means to you. Tape it or write it in your notebook or journal.
- Draw a stick figure of yourself and a thought bubble next to it. Inside the bubble, list three qualities about yourself that you are proud of and that make you unique.
- In what ways do you express your uniqueness when you're alone? With others? At work?
- Look through some old magazines and clip three or four pictures, images, words, or phrases that express how you feel when you let your light shine. Tape or glue them in your notebook or journal.

Faith Beyond Your Calling

At this hearth of faith, you will express your signature presence with the goal of being of service to others. This hearth connects your fire of faith to the Sacred Promise of legacy, the gift of service and stewardship. Social servant and politician Shirley Chisholm's life embodied her message: "Service is the rent we pay for room on this earth." As a steward of the future, your rent of service is the most important payment you'll ever make on behalf of this and future generations. Dr. Wangari Maathai, whom you met in Chapter Three, pays her rent of service by planting trees and educating others on ecological sustainability.

Service is at the heart of legacy living. It is up to you to choose what kind of service and for whom. If you already know what kind of service you'll offer, you'll need to match what you want to do with what is needed. If you don't know what or who you will serve, consider your goals. Also, ask yourself, "How do I like to spend my time? In what kind of activities? With what kind of people—adults, children?" Your answers will assist you in determining whom you want to serve and the kind of service you will offer.

Individuals who demonstrate faith beyond their calling through their service to others on behalf of the future include social, environmental, political, media, and spiritual leaders, such as Rosa Parks, Rachel Carson, Gandhi, Nelson Mandela, and Mother Teresa. Such individuals devote most if not all of their adult lives to tending this hearth of faith. At this hearth, you will hear the sound of your own voice saying, "I have faith in the future" and "I want to plant seeds that will nurture future generations for years to come." As demonstrated by Dr. Maathai, Vera, Joanne, Hank, Angelina, and others throughout this book, ordinary people just like you and me can also demonstrate this kind of extraordinary faith through our orientation to service and stewardship.

EXERCISES

Set aside time when you won't have any distractions, and remember to use your notebook or journal for your notes.

- Choose a person you admire who demonstrates faith beyond his or her calling on behalf of the future. Find a picture of that person and tape or glue it in your notebook or journal.
- List five things this person did or is doing in his or her service and stewardship. Choose one thing from your list and ask yourself, as a result of this person's stewardship, what will be different a year from now? How about ten years from now? Make a note about it.
- What have you done in the past to pay your rent of service?
- What would you enjoy doing now to pay your rent of service?

Faith Beyond Yourself

This hearth of faith connects you to a source of power that is higher, or greater, than ourselves. The many names for this higher source of power include Holy Spirit, Source, Spirit, the Divine, the Universe, Infinitude, the "still small voice" within, your inner compass. By whatever name, faith beyond yourself connects you to the benevolence and infinitude of that powerful source.

When you follow your own desires, you can easily go astray. When you surrender your desires to a higher source, you can stay connected to your highest calling. Throughout his years as champion for civil rights, Dr. Martin Luther King Jr. routinely received threatening phone calls. During the particularly tense days of the 1956 Montgomery Bus Boycott, Dr. King received a terrifying phone call that shook him to the core. Restless and unable to sleep, Dr. King prayed.

> I am here taking a stand for what I believe is right. But Lord, I must confess that I'm weak now, I'm faltering. I'm losing my courage. Now, I am afraid. . . . The people are looking for leadership, and if I stand before them without strength and courage, they too will falter. I am at the end of my powers. . . . I can't face it alone.

Later Dr. King described that time of prayer as an encounter with God unlike anything he had ever experienced. He recalled that it was as though he heard "the quiet assurance of an inner voice saying, 'Stand up for righteousness. . . . Stand up for truth. And lo, I will be with you. Even until the end of the world.'" Almost immediately, Dr. King's fears subsided. He says, "My uncertainty disappeared. I was ready to face anything."

As a teacher and public speaker, before I address an audience, I invoke the Sacred Promise of faith. Like Moses in the exodus from Egypt, through a simple prayer or invocation, I invite God's presence to precede me. By doing so, I become more conscious of the privilege afforded me as well as my immense responsibility as I stand in front of an audience. It also reminds me that I am not a vessel for my own ego or agenda but an ambassador of that higher source of divine grace.

AFFIRMATIONS: I'M DOING IT!

- I am courageous.
- I listen to and follow my inner voice and my inner compass.
- To arrive at someplace new, I am committed to stepping into the unknown.
- I understand that faith can connect me to a higher source outside of myself.
- I meditate or pray to invoke the power of a higher source.
- I understand that doubt, fear, and faith are connected.
- I am committed to successfully moving through my anxiety, doubt, and fear.

I BELIEVE IN YOU

Many years ago, when I was contemplating my doctoral thesis, I sought guidance from a leading scholar in two fields comprising my interdisciplinary degree, which included theater, linguistics, literature, and phenomenology. Dr. Bertrand Bronson was among the few scholars with the breadth and depth of knowledge that I needed to round out my dissertation committee. I wrote to invite him to be a member of my committee or, given his other commitments, one of my reviewers. Almost immediately, I received his reply. Because of his full schedule, Dr. Bronson graciously declined my request; he also included a grace note of encouragement, affirming my direction and progress. In so many words, he was saying, "Go for it! I believe in you."

Disappointed but undaunted, I forged ahead. I assembled the best professors to whom I had access for my dissertation committee. Though none of them had ever served on a committee for a thesis as complex as mine, they all had faith in me. On the winds of their and Dr. Bronson's confidence in my ability to carry out my research and make a worthwhile contribution to the field, I sailed through the sometimes choppy, chaotic waters of my research, writing, and defense of my thesis. I drew strength from the encouragement and support of my committee combined with faith in myself and God.

My faith was also shored up by an unexpected and unlikely source—Susan Sontag's small, contemplative, and groundbreaking book, *Illness as Metaphor.* For months, I pondered how I would pull the diverse threads of my research into a unified whole, a composition that would not consume several volumes. As I read and ruminated on this book about the nature and sources of illness, something shifted in me. Sontag's complex, controversial book offered me a model for what was possible, strengthening my faith that perhaps I, too, could achieve something comparable.

The Sacred Promise of faith offers the power of devotion and spiritual renewal. As you continue to exercise your muscles of faith, remember the four-sided hearth of faith. All sides are important as we tend to the fire of our true voice. Tend it well by spending time at all four sides of the hearth, giving each equal attention, so that the fire of your true voice is stoked and well lit to show the way for yourself and others. Take a moment now to reflect on how faith in yourself, faith in your own calling, faith beyond your calling, and faith beyond yourself are interconnected and how you can share your fire of faith in your life and pass the flame on to others.

> *Being faithful is more important than being*
> *successful. If we are successful in the world's*
> *eyes but unfaithful in terms of what we believe*
> *then we fail others.*
> MAX DEPREE

CHAPTER 6

Love—Passion and Heart-Centered Action

I am a little pencil in the hand of a writing God who is sending a love letter to the world.
MOTHER TERESA

MANY YEARS AGO, NANCY BAILEY WAS A SINGLE MOTHER on welfare with two young boys. Back then, her biggest goal was to get out of an abusive marriage to a drug dealer and provide for her sons, which she did. Though she struggled financially, her next goal was to get through college. After putting herself through college and graduate school, where she earned a Master's degree in clinical psychology, Nancy worked for many years as a substance-abuse counselor before going to work as a vice president for a bank, where she developed and directed their employee assistance program.

It seems that Nancy's calling has always been connected to caring for and assisting others.

> When I was fifteen or sixteen, my father asked me what I wanted to do when I grew up. To this day, I don't know where the idea came from or why, but I told him that I wanted to work with Indian women who lived in mud huts.

Little did Nancy know that as an adult, she would do exactly that. On a trip to Guatemala for a Spanish immersion program, her life dramatically changed when she visited an orphanage run by several nuns in the country's Western Highlands. In the orphanage, there were forty-five children, ages two to twelve. There was little adult supervision and no play activities for the children. When Nancy looked at their innocent faces and into their eyes, she knew they just wanted to be held and loved.

> I soon found myself covered with dirty, runny-nosed, lice-infested kids who found their way into my heart. When it was time to leave, I promised to come back and visit, but nobody believed me. The kids had been visited by many people who made the same promise, but they never came back.

Drawn by her love for children and a desire to help the children at this orphanage, Nancy did go back. She collected clothing, medicine, toys, and art supplies for the children and visited them every three months for four weeks at a time. After several trips, she realized that her four-week visits could never provide the type of help these kids so desperately needed: consistent, constant, limit-setting, caring adults in their lives and meaningful activities to stimulate their learning and creativity. After her sixth visit, Nancy decided to return to Guatemala to spend a year developing an enrichment program for the kids. Within a few months, however, she knew she could not leave the children and return to the United States.

In the fall of the following year, Nancy's life changed again.

> I greeted a young man who had come to the orphanage carrying a tiny bundle wrapped in towels. Thinking it was a loaf of bread, I peeked inside. Instead of bread, I found a baby girl. She was barely clinging to life.
>
> The baby was four days old and weighed only four pounds. The orphanage was not equipped to care for such a fragile child. Even though the doctor told me the baby would not likely survive, I took her home with me.

For several days, Nancy lovingly fed the baby with an eyedropper, and within a few days, she began to come around.

Shortly afterward, Nancy adopted the baby and named her Gabriela Maria.

Now in her teens, Gabriela is Nancy's constant reminder of the tremendous potential of children and is one of the reasons she founded Semillas de Amor ("seeds of love"), a grassroots organization dedicated to investing in Guatemalan children and their education. Nancy is the driving force behind the construction of the Semillas de Amor Children's Village, a home for children who are unable to remain with their biological families, a place where children are nurtured, given proper medical care, and allowed to blossom. Future plans for the Children's Village include a school, a clinic, and a day care facility for working mothers. Nancy's mission is "to provide care, high-level education, and solid futures for Guatemala's at-risk children."

Not long ago, Nancy described her encounter with one of the government officials whom she had contacted to get support for the Children's Village. For years, she has provided Gabriela with horseback-riding lessons and made sure that all the children of the Village had lessons. The government official didn't understand why Nancy would extend such generosity to orphans. Nancy couldn't see how she could do otherwise. She couldn't imagine giving her daughter more than the other children.

Nancy started her journey of the heart over fifteen years ago not knowing where it would lead, yet with faith that she was doing the right thing. That single step of faith was the creative action that launched her on her journey, followed by hundreds more creative actions. Nancy's love for herself, her children, and the children of the Semillas de Amor Children's Village is a testament to the Sacred Promise of love and the power of passion and heart-centered action. This promise also powerfully affirms that like Nancy, each of us is an artist. Your life is your great masterpiece. Each day you have an opportunity to paint on your canvas with the brushstrokes of your life. Painter and visual artist Jacob Lawrence puts it this way: "It is most important for an artist to develop an approach and philosophy about life. If he has developed this philosophy, he does not paint on canvas, he puts himself on canvas." The Sacred Promise of love invites you to put yourself on canvas by daring to paint and wear your soul on the outside.

EXPRESS YOUR LOVE

The vocabulary of love includes favor, esteem, attraction, desire, passion, playfulness, and rapture. Covering a diverse spectrum of emotion and experience, definitions of love vary widely, yet they all depend on one of three contexts, all of which are relational: **self-love**, **love for others**, and **Divine love**.

Self-Love

Focused on your relationship with yourself, self-love means holding yourself in high regard, knowing that you are an important and significant jewel in the crown of creation. It means loving yourself with the same intensity and immensity that we typically reserve for others. By leaving her abusive marriage, Nancy demonstrated self-love and, as a result, freed up an enormous storehouse of emotional, physical, mental, and spiritual energy for herself, her sons, and others. By this creative action, Nancy was able to draw more deeply from the well of her signature presence.

You demonstrate self-love when you say *yes* to yourself while saying *no* to someone else's agenda, so that you can stay on course with your calling. Self-love is when you can look in the mirror and honestly say that you love yourself unconditionally—regardless of your past, your background, your life circumstances. Self-love is the foundation for your love for others. The reality is that you cannot honor and love others unless you can honor, love, favor, and respect yourself. When you truly love yourself, the receipt of your creativity and creative actions will be tallied as follows:

- You see and acknowledge your inner and outer beauty.
- You set aside time for yourself.
- You are loyal to your calling by doing what you love and loving what you do.
- You say *yes* to and follow through on your commitments.
- You set and honor limits, constraints, and boundaries.
- You cultivate a playful heart and don't take yourself too seriously.
- You understand that love is the genesis, the source of your courage.

- You recognize that if you want significant change, you must begin with yourself.
- You reconnect with yourself and your calling through meditation, prayer, reading an uplifting book, listening to inspiring music, spending time in nature, seeking counsel from your circle of support.

As you prepare for the following *Questions for Reflection*, think about an occasion when you were positively joyous: celebrating a special birthday, being the first to make footprints or angels after a fresh snowfall, sighting a full rainbow after a storm, holding your child in your arms for the first time, holding your mother's hand to assist her in rising from her favorite chair.

QUESTIONS FOR REFLECTION

Set aside time when you won't have any distractions, and remember to use your notebook or journal for your notes.

- What does love mean to you?
- What is the rhythm, or presence, of love in your life?
- When has your head said *no* but your heart has said *yes?* List five examples. Circle the one that makes your heart sing!
- Who or what inspires you? The women, men, children, places, and ideas that inspire you can become teachers for you.
- Byllye Avery says that saying *no* as a complete sentence is self-love in action, particularly as it relates to others' agenda for you. Women tend to explain themselves when they say *no.* Often they talk themselves out of their *no* response instead of maintaining their ground. Under what circumstances do you say *no* as a complete sentence?
- In what ways do you celebrate yourself?

Love for Others

Love for others means you extend your love, concern, and caring toward someone or something other than yourself—including animals, places, our environment, as well as experiences and ideas. Love for others is about relating in a posture of service, consciously serving as a steward for others. You demonstrate this kind of love when you act on your goal to make a difference—however small or large—in someone else's life. Love for others declares, "I care about you, whether or not I know your name." Love for others says, "I understand that you and I are part of the same community, the same world. We need and depend on one another. I want to do what I can to make our community the best it can be and leave it a little bit better than it is now." This kind of love also says, "I choose to recycle paper goods and glass containers because I care about our environment."

You can express love for others by volunteering your services in your community, being an energy-conscious consumer, or donating gently used books, clothing, toys, and other resources so they can be used and enjoyed by others. You can also express this kind of love in many other ways, including these:

- Friendships and family relationships
- Commitment to a spouse or significant other
- Giving birth to and raising children, or by adopting or providing foster care
- Conscious care and stewardship of our streets, parks, forests, mountains, and waterways
- Excitement for new, innovative, and beneficial ideas
- Respect and caring for wild places, and for sanctuaries and other protected places
- Empathy and compassion for others, including people with whom you have no personal contact or relationship

In the tradition of the ages, Mother Teresa bids us to demonstrate our love for others not just through words but through our being, encouraging us to be "the loving expression of God's kindness." Mother Teresa reminds us to do what we can, while we can. "We are all but His instruments who do our little bit and pass by." As an instrument called to exude kindness, let it flow through you—your eyes, your countenance, your whole being—not only in what you do for others, but also in the way in which you do it.

EXERCISES

Set aside time when you won't have any distractions, and remember to use your notebook or journal for your notes.

- Create a collage that focuses on being of service to others. Remember that "others" include people, our environment, animals, experiences, and ideas. Look through a stack of old magazines, newspapers, or Internet articles. Take fifteen to twenty minutes to clip images, stories, advertisements, quotations, words, and anything else that catches your eye. Don't take time to think about what you're clipping, just follow your intuition. Set aside an hour or so to create your collage. Use your notebook or journal or a separate piece of paper. Give your collage a title.
- A simple way to practice love for others is to let kindness flow through you. This portable two-part exercise will take about five minutes.

    1. When you are free from distractions, take a few moments to notice your breath. Breathe in and hold your breath for a count of three. Let it go. Repeat several times.
    2. Now, recall a time when someone said a kind word or did something kind for you. Allow this feeling of kindness to flow through your eyes, your mouth, your arms and legs, your whole body. Now you are ready to breathe kindness in and out. As you breathe in, recall your memory of kindness. Hold this memory and your breath for a count of three. Now breathe this memory of kindness out. Repeat several times.

This exercise is a great stress-reliever, a gift of self-love and love for others. Once you get the feel of it, you can let kindness flow through you at home, work, or anywhere.

Divine Love

Divine love is the quality of love that extends beyond the cognitive, emotional, and physical realms into wonder, awe, and mystery. Divine love is experienced in the breathtaking depths of the Grand Canyon, the great expanse and terrifying beauty of the white thunder of Niagara Falls, the magnitude of the engineering triumphs of the great pyramids of Mexico and Egypt. Divine love is experienced in the profound vision, artistry, craftsmanship, and sacredness of a magnificent cathedral—interior and exterior—not to mention the approach. On my first visit to Chartres Cathedral, I approached by train from the west. From at least ten miles away, the great cathedral loomed above the picturesque, sparsely populated French countryside. Drawn into her glorious embrace, I was mesmerized, transfixed, and blessed by a particular kinship with so many others who throughout the ages were welcomed as pilgrims there. Such experiences of wonder, awe, and mystery are massage therapy for your soul. Beyond nourishing your soul, these experiences of divine love spark creativity that will flow into other areas of your life.

Understanding that love and creativity are as one, Picasso rightly observes that "we are seized by both in encounter." Divine love is intimately related to creativity, for it connects us to all creation, including the great Creator. This kind of love is also connected to honoring your God-given gifts. When you express your love through your creativity, you honor the highest and deepest aspects of your own divinity, showing reverence for the source of your creativity. You also express your deep affinity with the Divine by honoring your true nature, your true voice.

Divine love encourages and challenges you to

- Pay attention to beauty, wonder, and mystery—a magical moonrise that pours slant light across a darkening meadow, birds flocking together, a soulful symphony of soundless flight
- Use your creativity to imagine and dream, knowing that what you construct is the visible, tangible work of your heart, hands, and creative spirit
- Know that your creativity is needed by a friend, relative, coworker, or stranger whose name you may never know

- Know that someone is depending on you—you will make a difference; you already have by honoring your creativity
- Take your skills and talents seriously, which means that you not only honor but also continuously hone your skills and talents because they are your gift to the world
- Remember who you are, which means that you remember God's legacy for you

EXERCISES

Set aside time when you won't have any distractions, and remember to use your notebook or journal for your notes.

- Light a candle. Put on your favorite soul-soothing music. Draw a bouquet of your favorite flowers. Color them with crayons, markers, or colored pencils.
- Write a letter expressing your love for someone or something—an experience, an encounter, an idea that you consider to be exquisitely beautiful, wonderful, or awe inspiring. As you write, let your love flow. Express yourself exuberantly, joyously. If you feel comfortable doing so, begin your letter by addressing God. When you're finished, read your letter aloud.
- Make a copy of your letter and carry it with you in your briefcase, wallet, or pocket. Read your letter frequently to rekindle the love you expressed.

Nancy Bailey, whom we met earlier in this chapter, embodies love in its diverse contexts. Self-love gave Nancy the emotional and spiritual fortitude to leave her husband, which meant that she could invest more time and energy in building a better future for herself and for her sons. Nancy's love for others is evident in how she raised her sons, her employee-assistance work in the corporate world, her vision for and creation of Semillas de Amor Children's Village, and how she poured herself into her adopted daughter, Gabriela, and the many other little ones at the Children's Village.

All of Nancy's creative actions of self-love and love for others are also manifestations of Divine love, highlighted by Nancy's imaginative, heart-centered vision and the tangible work of her heart. Nancy's peeking into the blanket and discovering Gabriela and not a loaf of bread, as well as her creation of the Children's Village, embody Kahlil Gibran's message that "Work is love made visible." Your work can also be love made visible. And like Nancy Bailey, when you live with passionate intention and let your light shine through your signature presence, you too can experience the difference that only you can make in your own and others' lives.

THE FACES OF LOVE

As an undergraduate at the University of Michigan, I had the good fortune to enroll in a poetry course taught by Robert Hayden, literary scholar, activist, and poet. Because Hayden viewed himself through the lens of humanity and not through the constricting lens of race, I hesitate to use the epithet African-American to refer to any of his attributes and distinguished achievements. If he would lay claim to any other attribution, it would be as a devotee to his Baha'i faith, which sustained him through years of struggle and virtual obscurity. Throughout his life, Hayden embodied and demonstrated the immense power of passionate intention.

During that precious year that I studied with Hayden, I learned much from him. Through his unflagging devotion to poetry, I learned about the many faces of love. Through his unflinching integrity, I learned about his character. Through both, I learned how to stand still and stay focused on one's true love, even in the face of resistance, intolerance, and obscurity.

Hayden's true love was poetry. His reverence for poetic form and language reigned supreme. His poetic brilliance, luminous spirit, and understanding of love's complexities are empathetically articulated in his sonnet "Those Winter Sundays":

> Sundays too my father got up early
> and put his clothes on in the blueblack cold,
> then with cracked hands that ached
> from labor in the weekday weather made

banked fires blaze. No one ever thanked him.
I'd wake and hear the cold splintering, breaking.
When the rooms were warm, he'd call,
and slowly I would rise and dress,
fearing the chronic angers of that house,
speaking indifferently to him,
who had driven out the cold
and polished my good shoes as well.
What did I know, what did I know
of love's austere and lonely offices?

We will never know if this poignant poem is about the love for the man who took Hayden into his heart and home by adopting him when he was a babe in arms. We do know that the poem is about the quality of love unexpressed and expressed in the face and tug of life's daily routines.

One of the things I remember most about Hayden, who was legally blind, is his face. Behind his glasses, whose thickness distorted his eyes and for which many students mocked him behind his back, I remember Hayden's face because I experienced his emotions and spirit through his eyes, mouth, and facial expressions. When he read my poems, in order to see the words, he held the page within an inch or so of his face. As though his hand and his heart were touching mine, I cherished this closeness, welcoming the presence of a familiar, not in the flesh but in the soul. Hayden always read poems two or three times, first for sense and then for what he called the music and soul of the poem. And as he breathed my words into life, I watched the lightweight onion-skin paper undulate with the rise and fall of his breath. Behind the paper curtain, his face hidden and emotions, too, behind the veil of his almost monotone voice, I always wondered, *what is he thinking?* And more important, *what is he feeling?* Standing very close to see me with whatever clarity he could, he'd pull the paper down to offer feedback about my poem. Only then did I feel the fullness of his exuberant emotions, his excitement, surprise, anger, or frustration. And always his abiding hope and joy.

Robert Hayden's legacy is evident not only in his love of language, but also in his steadfast self-love. By refusing to align himself with the poets of the Black Arts Movement, who favored free verse and political tropes to signify their resistance, Hayden's use of conventional poetic meter and forms situated his work then and now within the broader canon and the more enduring traditions of English poetry. For me and many other poets, Hayden's unshakable devotion to poetry and to himself continues to instruct and inform our practice. Through these loves, he honored the past even as he broke away from the old. And wearing a robe of possibility, he reached out to a new generation of poets, showing us through his work and life what we might strive for and achieve.

We all wear robes of possibility. At the heart of it, the Sacred Promise of love is about falling in love with yourself so that you will fully embrace your possibility. This means holding yourself in high regard and saying *yes* to what matters to *you*, dealing with distractions when someone or something attempts to sabotage your agenda, and falling in love with the future so that you can devote your emotional, physical, intellectual, and spiritual energy to be of service to yourself and to others.

Nancy Bailey and Robert Hayden show us what is possible through the power of love and heart-centered action. Nancy directed her passionate intention toward helping herself and others, particularly focusing on children as the face of her love. Similarly, by focusing on his true love, Hayden exemplified passionate intention. And though his work was not widely read or appreciated during his lifetime, his poetry now continues to gain the recognition it deserves along with his growing influence on poets of current and future generations.

My father used to say that love is the only thing that multiplies when you give it away, especially when you give love freely and joyously. As you consider the many ways you express your love for yourself, for others, and in appreciating and contributing to the beauty that's all around you, remember to honor your heart and say an emphatic *yes* to what matters to you, so that you will wear your robe of possibility for what you truly love. For when you honor your true love and express it with passionate intention, your love will also serve others in the here and now and into the future.

AFFIRMATIONS: I'M DOING IT!

- I follow my passion and calling, doing what I love and loving what I do.
- I organize my life around my calling.
- I am committed to a cause that I passionately believe in.
- I lose track of time when I'm doing something I love.
- I make a note of people who inspire me.
- I follow through on my commitments.
- I am an ally or guide for others.
- I freely share my joy with others.
- I care about my own well-being and that of others, regardless of whether I know them personally.
- I am using my signature presence to be of service to others.
- I routinely seek people, places, ideas, and experiences that inspire me.
- I recognize the beauty and nobility in all people, things, and places.
- I am open to awe, mystery, the sacred, and the Divine.

Helping out is not some special skill. It is not the domain of rare individuals. It is not confined to a single part or time of our lives. We simply heed the call of that natural caring impulse within, and follow where it leads us.
RAM DASS

CHAPTER 7

Vision—Seeing the Bigger Picture

*When I dare to be powerful—to use my strength in
the service of my vision, then it becomes less and less
important whether I am afraid.*
AUDRE LORDE

FOR JEFF BEZOS, FOUNDER AND CEO OF AMAZON.COM, vision is
everything. Seeing the big picture, taking the long view, and
spotting and leveraging both short- and long-term opportunities comes naturally. Since its inception in 1995, Amazon has led
the way among online retailers. Bezos's vision, combined with
his exceptional ability for selling standard products in ways that
anticipate and satisfy customer needs, helped Amazon turn the
retail book market on its head virtually overnight, and it has been
raising the bar ever since. Because of Bezos's vision of what was
possible, customers around the world enjoy easy, 24/7 access to
an unprecedented selection of books, music, videos, games, toys,
consumer electronics, and an array of other merchandise.

In dynamic, competitive environments, a company's competitive advantage often hinges on internal resourcefulness and flexibility. As head of Amazon, Bezos cultivates and nurtures a culture
of inclusion and innovation. He and a cadre of senior leaders
called the "S Team" set and drive strategy. They also know that to
maintain their success and competitive edge, the responsibility for
the company's vision and strategy must cascade and be appropriately scaled at all levels throughout the organization. For example,

the person who oversees the Web service that allows third parties to take advantage of Amazon's vast network of fulfillment centers must, while thinking and acting strategically for his part of the business, keep in mind the context of the company's overall vision.

Bezos is known for his ability to take the long view, which provides the necessary context for growth and innovation. As Julia Kirby and Thomas Stewart point out in their excellent article "The Institutional Yes," a fundamental and prized aspect of Amazon's culture is their willingness to plant seeds coupled with the patience to wait for those seeds to sprout, come to fruition, and have a meaningful return on investment. In their business, this can take anywhere from five to seven years. Within the context of their overarching vision, Amazon's ability to take the long view allows them the enviable advantage to explore and plant seeds for new ventures while expanding and making the core business even more productive and cost-efficient.

LIVE YOUR VISION

Whether it is connected to an organization, such as Amazon, your relationships with family, friends, and coworkers, or to you personally, a compelling vision is a galvanizing force. Just like you, a vision is vibrant and alive, constantly growing and evolving. When connected to your calling, your deepest passions, and your core values, vision is the powerful magnet that draws your own and others' energy toward your desired future.

Do not confuse your calling and your vision because, though related, they are also quite distinct. Your calling, which we discussed very early in the book, is solely focused on your vocation, that special work that you feel you *must* do. You feel it so strongly that you believe your life would be incomplete without it. Calling is all about listening to and following your inner compass or, if you believe in God, listening to and following His call on your life.

By contrast, vision is broader than calling. Whereas your calling is about doing work that is right for you, vision is about recognizing the diverse areas of your life, which includes your work life, or your calling, but also extends far beyond. Your calling will be one of the many elements of your vision—in addition to your personal life, family life, social life, and leisure life. When I work with my clients, they include all of these elements in their vision. Many also include their health, well-being, and spiritual life.

Vision is about ensuring that you reach your fullest potential and live a balanced life, integrating all the areas of your life to meet your needs. Because your needs evolve depending on your life stage, goals, and so on, your vision will also be fluid and dynamic.

Vision's magnetic power keeps you aligned with your future despite the prevailing winds of negativity, inertia, inadequacy, and insufficiency that conspire to hold you back, keeping you tethered to the same habits, relationships, or work that no longer serve you, your best interests, or the common good.

The Sacred Promise of vision invites you to engage your outer and inner ways of seeing and knowing and to begin a process of deep transformation. For when you can see and appreciate the truth of current reality and focus on a compelling future, you set the wheels in motion to change what is to what can be. You embark upon a journey that will transform your life. Vision is the bridge that connects you to the future, for it allows you to hold in your mind's eye, heart, and soul images of your passion. Expressing vision is to fall in love with the future. You fall in love with the future by envisioning or imagining what you want to create.

Before you begin the next set of *Questions for Reflection,* take a moment to consider how you see the world around you. Do you see it as open and receptive? Harsh and demanding? Easy and generous? How you see the world around you affects how you see yourself and how you shape your personal vision.

QUESTIONS FOR REFLECTION

Set aside time when you won't have any distractions, and remember to use your notebook or journal for your notes.

- What does vision mean to you?
- What is the rhythm, or presence, of vision in your life?
- What insights from your past can help you envision how you want to live now and in the future? Reflect on your childhood and answer these questions:

    1. Did you grow up in a big city or a small town?

2. What are your favorite memories of your family, school, pets, friends, vacations?
3. What were some of your favorite activities?

TWO ASPECTS OF VISION

To shape and live your vision, you must understand two crucial aspects of it. The most familiar aspect is concerned with the future and dwells in the language of desire, aspiration, imagination, hope, dreams, and possibility. This aspect of vision offers an enticing glimpse into the mansion of tomorrow—yours—and opens wide its doors to allow the invigorating air of possibility to claim you. In her inimitable way, Emily Dickinson paints in the following poem an ephemeral yet tantalizing portrait of this future-oriented facet of vision, a picture worthy of your legacy as you envision the realm of possibility for yourself.

> I dwell in Possibility—
> A fairer House than Prose—
> More numerous of Windows—
> Superior—for Doors—
>
>
> Of Chambers as the Cedars—
> Impregnable of Eye—
> And for an Everlasting Roof
> The Gambrels of the Sky—
>
>
> Of Visitors—the fairest—
> For Occupation—This—
> The spreading wide my narrow Hands
> To gather Paradise—

In contrast to the enticing paradise of possibility, the second aspect of vision is grounded in the present. It lives in the language of the here and now, the language of current reality: our crowded or half-empty calendars, our over- or under-committed lives, our lost, missed, or yet to be imagined opportunities. In the process of creating a vision that will transform your life, you must take stock of where you are in the here and now by clearly assessing your current reality. You might be tempted to gloss over this step in favor of the more glamorous and seductive task of creating your vision of your future reality—painting on the canvas of your desired future, or as Dickinson says, "spreading wide" your "narrow Hands / To gather Paradise." However, if you ignore current reality, you will do so at great peril to yourself in the here and now and in achieving whatever you want to create in the future.

To begin the process of deep transformation, not only must you open your hands and heart toward the paradise that beckons, but you must also have a very clear grasp of current reality as you maintain your purchase on the solid ground of the present. Inspired by Andrew Wyeth's evocative painting of the same name, my poem "Christina's World" honors and salutes the dynamic tension between current reality and a vision of the future.

> In that brown
> and grassy sea,
> everything depends
> on her arm,
> bony, pink, and turned
> just so.
>
> One hand tethered
> irretrievably
> to earth's dark knoll.
> The other a sea bird,
> open-winged, ever seeking
> that marvelous, miraculous
> frenzy of flight.

As you are pulled toward the allure of your desired future, your key task and challenge will be to hold on to your future vision while simultaneously living the daily ups and downs of your current reality on "earth's dark knoll." You will know that your vision has holding power when it comes from your heart—and then you will be engaged and have the power to engage others.

CONSTRUCT YOUR DESIRED FUTURE

There are many ways to identify and assemble the building blocks to create your desired future. For individual clients and in my workshops, I often use the approach outlined in the next *Sample Exercise*. For organizational clients, I adapt this exercise to meet the particular "story" that lives within every corporation, university, law firm, faith and civic institution. For now, I invite you to simply read through the exercise. Later in this chapter, I will provide an exercise specifically for you to begin assembling the building blocks to construct your desired future.

SAMPLE EXERCISE

I invite my client to imagine his or her life as a book with many chapters in it. I say, "The chapters of your life's book will capture highlights of your life. I invite you to recall some of the highlights of your past, present, and future. Be sure to consider the various stages of your life and include the following."

- Delights and disappointments of your childhood
- Odyssey of your teenage years and your transition into early adulthood
- Intimate eddies of friendships that mature perhaps into enduring relationships with others, including a primary relationship with your spouse or partner
- Peaks and valleys of family life, such as having and raising children, or deciding not to have children
- Choices you've made for your work and career
- Transition into midlife, productive retirement, and preparation for the passage beyond

To prepare for the next step in this exercise, I say, "The chapters in your book are animated by three central themes that shape each of our lives whether or not we are consciously aware of them: *Who am I now? Who am I becoming? Where am I going?* These themes are significant because beneath their surface is the story of your life. Your response to these and related questions will awaken powerful subconscious energies and bring them to the surface of your awareness.

"If you do not bring these energies to consciousness, if you permit them to remain underground as most of us do, they will propel you anyway, sometimes with unexpected consequences.

"The undesirable consequences take on myriad manifestations, including resignation, giving in to others' agendas rather than your own, projection, boredom, alienation, behavioral challenges such as lying to yourself and others, blaming others and feeling victimized rather than assuming authority and sovereignty over your life.

"The positive consequences include recognizing what has heart and meaning for you, what brings you joy, what new project, idea, or person is calling to you at this time in your life, and what might be holding you back so that you can effectively deal with it and move on toward your vision."

I invite my client to review the highlights of his or her life thus far and to write down some of the highlights. I say, "Write without stopping, if you can, for an hour."

CLEAR THE FOG

Most of us travel through life in a fog, unable or unwilling to see ourselves clearly. The previous sample exercise is specifically designed to help clear the fog, so that you can take up the invitation of the Sacred Promise of vision, which invites you to slow down long enough to reflect on and get clarity about what is important to you so that you can make positive, life-affirming choices and live with passionate intention.

Who am I now? Who am I becoming? Where am I going? Though you might have known the answers to these questions at one time in your life, perhaps you've reached a point where you are ready to reconsider where you have been, who you are and what now matters to you, who you are becoming, and where you are going. Perhaps you have graduated from college, traveled or worked for several years, and are ready to consider what's next for you. Perhaps you've raised your children and are ready for a new focus in your life. Maybe you're looking for what's important to you as you consider a new job, a new relationship, or the next phase of your life. Whatever the reasons, the Sacred Promise of vision offers a place to begin, or a place to continue a process that is already under way. This promise offers you a way to see your current circumstances with clarity and decide what creative action you will take to transform your life so that the magnet of vision pulls you toward your destiny, your desired future reality.

ASSESS YOUR CURRENT REALITY

To assess your current reality, you must address some important questions. The sets of *Questions for Reflection* on the following pages are linked. In *Questions for Reflection: Part One*, you will focus only on your *current* reality, which relates to the bigger question *Who am I now?* In *Questions for Reflection: Part Two*, you will focus only on your *future* reality, which relates to the bigger questions *Who am I becoming? Where am I going?* Sequence doesn't matter. You can do either part first. It does matter that you complete both sets of questions. If you plan to complete both sets in one sitting, be sure to give yourself plenty of time (allow three to four hours). You also could do one set of questions one day and the other set in another day or so. No matter which approach you choose, give yourself plenty of time to reflect on, ponder, and examine each question. This is your life!

QUESTIONS FOR REFLECTION: PART ONE

Set aside time when you won't have any distractions, and remember to use your notebook or journal for your notes.

The questions below will help you to assess your *current reality*. All of them relate to the bigger question *Who am I now?*

Answer all the questions honestly and completely. If you simply go through the motions, the questions will be a nice diversion, but they won't be very useful to you. If some questions seem too difficult to answer, don't worry. That's OK—for now. Go on to the next question and at a later time come back to those you skipped. Often the most difficult questions are the most revealing and useful as you assess your current reality.

As you reflect on each question, remember to be gentle with yourself. Pay attention to what gets stirred up and aroused in you, because this is your soul daring to speak to you, using the language of love and desire, blessing and thanksgiving, faith and confidence. As your soul speaks to you, pay attention to its desires and remember to listen with your heart, for when you do, your soul will continue to speak. If you listen only with your head, you might not hear your soul's whisperings.

If this is the first time you have seen or answered questions like these, congratulate yourself for taking a step that most people have never taken before, as you are about to embark on the most important expedition of your life.

- What five qualities do you like most about yourself? Why?
- What three qualities would you change about yourself? Why?
- When you were a child, who were two or three people you admired? Jot down their names and why you admired them.
- When you were a child, who or what had the greatest influence on you?
- When you were a child, what did you want to be or do when you grew up?
- What sayings or teachings do you recall from when you were a young person? Are they meaningful to you now?
- How would you describe yourself? Would your best friend describe you in the same way? If not, what would be different?
- What are you here for? Why do you exist? In other words, what is your mission, your purpose, your highest calling in life?
- Are you happy with your life as it is now?

If you were writing a story about your life, your answers to the first set of *Questions for Reflection* would form an outline of your current reality to assist you in fleshing out the rich details of your life. Similarly, if you were painting a picture, your answers would be the beginning brushstrokes of your magnificent self-portrait.

Before you go on further in this chapter, take time to read and reflect on your responses; then give your story outline or self-portrait a title that resonates for you. Your title might be simple and straightforward: "My Current Reality." It might be more descriptive. Here are some examples of titles from my coaching clients: "My Life and Welcome to It," "Standing at the Edge of Salmon Creek," "The Way It Is," and "I'd Rather Be Climbing Stone Mountain." Make a note of your title for your story outline or self-portrait in your journal or notebook. Put today's date next to it.

IMAGINE YOUR FUTURE REALITY

If you want to transform your current reality, you must be able to envision your future reality. To be meaningful and have pulling and staying power, your vision must be bigger than you, encouraging you to reach beyond yourself to create a more compelling and worthy future.

The *Questions for Reflection: Part Two* are linked to the first set of questions. They will help you take stock of *who you are becoming* and *where you are going*. Your answers to these questions will not only provide insights to what is most significant for you, your responses will help you get a clearer vision of your future reality, of who you are becoming and where you are headed. Your answers may also point to areas of your signature presence that you have overlooked; gifts, talents, or aspirations that you may want to revive; wounds or areas in your life that need healing or closure; fears or places where you are stuck and must confront so that they release their powerful grip on you; opportunities for growth that beckon you to add depth and richness to your life that may be missing from your current reality.

QUESTIONS FOR REFLECTION: PART TWO

Set aside time when you won't have any distractions, and remember to use your notebook or journal for your notes.

The questions below will help to assess your *future reality*. All of them relate to the bigger questions *Who am I becoming? Where am I going?* Remember to answer all the questions honestly and completely: be gentle with yourself; pay attention to what your soul says to you; and congratulate yourself for taking the next step in your vision work.

- What are you most proud of about yourself and your accomplishments?
- What are three peak moments or experiences in your life?
- Describe one of these peak moments or experiences in detail. When did it happen? Who was there with you? How did you feel? What did you say? What did others say?
- What are your strengths? How will they serve you in the future?
- If you were living life to your highest potential, what contribution would you be making to your family? Your job? Your community? Your world?
- Are you in good health? Is your health optimal? If not, what resources or support do you need to maintain a healthy lifestyle?
- With whom or on what issues do you avoid conflict? Is your avoidance connected to a fear, something you would rather not acknowledge?
- If you could change three things about your life, what would you change? Why? What's stopping you?
- Do you have a fulfilling hobby? If so, what is it? If not, write down three things you enjoy doing and that you would consider including in your life.
- Do you help others or volunteer in your community?
- What are you doing for others that you want to continue doing?

(Continued)

- How might you make a difference in someone else's life?
- What is your plan for ongoing personal growth and development?

If you were writing a story about your life, your answers to the second set of questions would form an outline to assist you in fleshing out the rich details of your life *as you want it to be*. If you were painting a picture, your answers would be the beginning brushstrokes of your self-portrait *as you see yourself in the future*.

Before you move further in this chapter, take time to read and reflect on your responses, then give your story outline or self-portrait of your future reality a title that resonates for you. Your title might be simple and straightforward: "My Future Reality." It might be more descriptive. Here are some examples of titles from individuals in my workshops: "Living Green and Loving It!" "Begin with the End in Mind," and "Angels Are Watching Over Me." Make a note of your title for your story outline or self-portrait in your journal or notebook. Put today's date on it.

Congratulations! You have completed two "snapshots" of *who you are now* and *who you are becoming*! Your creative actions are significant. They will help you clear the fog and create a solid foundation for your future vision.

The act of envisioning is one of many steps in the process of transformation, of realizing and manifesting your new reality so that you can wear your soul on the outside. Look closely at each set of responses that form your story outlines or self-portraits of your current and future realities. Without judging what you created, look for similarities and differences between your responses for the two sets of questions. The differences are key because they will point the way to transformation. The differences between your story outlines or self-portraits will provide the clarity that says: *This is who I am now. This is what I care about now. And this is who I want to become. This is where I am headed.*

To realize your new vision, you must feel a much stronger pull toward your future reality than you do from your current reality. In his book *Creating*, Robert Fritz calls this pull *creative tension*. If the creative tension is too weak, you won't generate sufficient momentum to escape the powerful pull of your current reality to propel *and* sustain you in moving toward your future vision. It helps to think of the enormous energy a rocket requires to escape the powerful pull of Earth's gravity. Your future vision must have that kind of powerful pull on the personal gravity of your current reality. Let's face it, even if our current reality stinks, most people prefer what they know to what they don't. Unless there is sufficient tension between your current reality (your present state) and your future reality (your envisioned outcome), you will remain in the relative comfort zone of your current reality.

CREATE YOUR VISION MAP

Your story outlines or self-portraits of your current and future reality would be incomplete without some kind of map that points the way to realizing your vision. Your vision map will identify the terrain that you must navigate to travel the distance between *here* and *there*, providing you with a high-level view of where you want to go.

You can create your vision map in words or visual images. You might create it as an outline, several paragraphs that form the skeleton of a story of your future reality, a story with you as author and main character. Or you might create a drawing, a sequence of photos, a collage of compelling images that have specific relevance and meaning for you. Just today, one of my clients who is a depth psychologist sent me a vibrantly colored pen-and-ink drawing. After months of considering options for her future, Pamela experienced a breakthrough, which she beautifully rendered in her drawing. For Pamela, her drawing comprised the contours of her future vision. This was her highly personal version of the map that charts the landscape of the next phase of her life.

Whether you create your vision map in words or visual images, it will be a highly personal declaration of what you care about and where you are headed. Begin with the familiar, a list or an outline perhaps, but do not constrain or limit yourself to the kind of process that is most familiar to you. Challenge yourself to find a new form, a new approach, a new way to create your vision map. Express yourself. Be creative. Experiment. Get out of the box. You will be glad you did.

As you embark on the road to your vision, remember that the map is not the territory. To get from *here* to *there*, from your current reality to wearing your soul on the outside in your future reality, you'll need more than a vision and vision map. You'll also need the resources of the Sacred Promises that you learned about in earlier chapters—gratitude, faith, and love—as well as the resources that you will learn about in the next few chapters, the Sacred Promises of integrity, creative action, and legacy.

The Sacred Promise of vision connects your calling to your future. It helps you clear the fog so that you can see where you are in your current reality and where you are headed. This promise invites you take up residence in the house of possibility, where you will find that in place of the obstacles or walls you have had in your life, new windows and doors will open. New rooms will appear. Entirely new vistas await you.

AFFIRMATIONS: I'M DOING IT!

- I keep a journal.
- I am clear about my calling and know where I am going.
- I am a keen observer.
- I routinely set aside time to reflect on matters that are important to me.
- I routinely look at people and situations with a fresh perspective.
- I am intentional about setting a specific passionate intention each day.
- I am passionate about my vision.
- I focus most of my time and energy on creating a compelling future.
- I know my next steps.
- I am committed to holding on to my vision even though others may not see it yet.

> *What lies behind us and what lies before us are tiny matters compared to what lies within us.*
> RALPH WALDO EMERSON

CHAPTER 8

Integrity—Honoring Your Values and Wholeness

*Each time a man stands up for an ideal, or acts
to improve the lot of others, or strikes out against
injustice, he sends forth a tiny ripple of hope, and
crossing each other from a million different centers
of energy and daring, those ripples can build a
current which can sweep down the mightiest walls
of oppression and resistance.*
ROBERT F. KENNEDY

FROM HIS HUMBLE BEGINNINGS to his ascent to the White House during the most divisive time in the history of the United States, Abraham Lincoln was known for his honesty and integrity. An American legend, his life continues to instruct us today. Born in a tiny, one-room log cabin in the Kentucky backwoods, he taught himself to read by candlelight. Through his own intelligence and efforts, and with the encouragement of his loving stepmother to continuously improve himself, Lincoln grew up to be a man of indisputable character and the greatest leader the American people have ever known.

By his own estimation, Lincoln received only one year of formal education. But with hard work and perseverance, he was elected to the Illinois legislature and admitted to the Illinois bar.

After a successful law career and a term as United States Representative, Lincoln set his sights on the country's highest office. Given the prevailing standards of the day and Lincoln's background and history, he was an unlikely presidential candidate. With his gangly physical appearance, frontier accent, down-home wit, and unassuming manner, he was often mocked publicly and behind his back. However, through his deep caring for his fellow man, his fierce commitment to his country, and his honesty and integrity, he won the confidence of the American people.

Though he lost his bid for the Senate against Stephen Douglas, during a series of debates with him, Lincoln demonstrated his passionate concern for those enslaved, his empathy for slaveholders, and his unwavering commitment to the preservation of the Union. Two years after these debates, Lincoln would be president, taking on the formidable task of holding together the Union during the Civil War, using his remarkable ability to take a clear position and simultaneously hold opposing points of view. According to Lincoln scholar and author Doris Kearns Goodwin, one of the secrets to Lincoln's political genius was that, unlike his political rivals, Lincoln commanded extraordinary emotional strengths. And though Lincoln battled depression throughout his life, author Joshua Shenks asserts that Lincoln's melancholy fueled his greatness. Goodwin's illuminating book, *Team of Rivals*, describes what she calls Lincoln's "first-class emotional intelligence," which enabled him to see into the hearts of his rivals and manage to eventually win their allegiance and support.

Unlike many of his contemporaries, Lincoln understood and spoke this truth to the American people: the Union could not "endure permanently half-slave and half-free," and throughout the tumult of the war, he remained focused and true to what he saw as his sacred duty: preserving the Union. Lincoln's friend and law partner, William H. Herndon, offered this fitting tribute:

> Although he cared little for simple facts, rules, and methods, it was on the underlying principle of truth and justice that Lincoln's will was firm as steel and tenacious as iron. . . . When justice, right, liberty, the government, the Constitution, the Union, humanity were involved, then you may all stand aside. No man can move him. No set of men can.

Lincoln's challenge to hold together a nation in jeopardy of being torn asunder mirrors our challenge at an individual level. Though absolutely different in intensity and scale, Lincoln confronted the same threshold that you and I face at the personal level, which is to live undivided, intact, whole.

HONOR YOUR INTEGRITY

All of us are born whole. On our journey toward adulthood, our wholeness gradually erodes, flaking away in the course of daily living. Erosion begins in our family system. In that weather, however gentle or harsh, we learn what and whom to value, what is safe and what is too risky, what is rewarded and what is reprimanded. As children, most of us want to please, and so it becomes quite easy to surrender our natural inclinations and ways of being to the wishes and whims of well-meaning parents, siblings, and members of our extended family. Each surrender can engender another until it sometimes becomes easier to adapt and relinquish ourselves than to stand our ground and preserve our authentic nature. In no time at all, it seems, we develop the acuity to adapt our behavior so that we can transform our father's or mother's sigh of resignation into a smile of encouragement, taking the first steps down the long road that will ultimately put greater distance between our true self and our adaptive, or false, self. We become so adept at adopting the agendas set by others, we lose track of our own agenda, our own inner compass, our own North Star.

The essential tasks and challenges of the Sacred Promise of integrity are claiming, embracing, and reintegrating those aspects of yourself that have eroded or become otherwise hidden to you over time. On the road to integrity, your ultimate destination is **wholeness**, one of three dimensions of integrity. Along this road, you will also encounter two additional dimensions of integrity—**honesty** and **congruence**. All of these aspects of the Sacred Promise of integrity are demonstrated in Abraham Lincoln's remarkable life.

Integrity and Honesty

In its most common usage, integrity means to be honest, with yourself and others. Being honest means that you speak your truth by saying what is so, or true, for you. Not only do you say what is true; you must also *be* what is true for you. True in the sense of being aligned with your inner spiritual compass. When you are true to your inner compass, this dimension of integrity is an ally that keeps you on track with your calling, as we learned about in earlier encounters with Andrea Bocelli, Nancy Bailey, and others.

Being honest also means that you stand up for what you believe, as Abraham Lincoln did, even when it might be unpopular to do so. Honesty is the aspect of integrity that says, "I am true to myself. I am loyal to what I believe. These are my values. Here's where I stand, what I stand for, and whom I stand with." You offer refreshing assurance that says, "I'm trustworthy, true to my word. You can count on me to say what I'll do and do what I say." The people you spend time with don't have to wonder where you're coming from because you are open with them.

On the path of legacy living, as you wear your soul on the outside, you will confront the counterparts to honesty, which show up as dishonesty, deceit, self-deception, betrayal, and so on. These are all aspects of the false self—the self that you want others to know and like so you can fit in, get along, or belong. In this no-win game, you pretend to be different from the real you: you hide out, hold back, pretend to be less than or more than you really are, dimmer or brighter, sadder or happier. The antidote to dishonesty? Honesty.

QUESTIONS FOR REFLECTION

Set aside time when you won't have any distractions, and remember to use your notebook or journal for your notes.

- What does this aspect of integrity—honesty—mean to you?
- What is the rhythm, or presence, of honesty in your life?
- What do you believe in? Do others know your beliefs?
- Do you talk openly about yourself with others?

Integrity and Congruence

Integrity requires you to be congruent in what you say and what you do; you must walk your talk. When you stand and walk with integrity, your actions match what you say you believe and value. This was certainly true for Lincoln. As his friend and law partner attests, Lincoln was unmovable on such high-stakes issues as justice, liberty, and humanity. For Lincoln, aligning his actions with his values was as necessary and natural as breathing.

Our word *value* is from the French *valoir*, which means "to be worth." Your values express what is of worth to you. Your family, friends, and coworkers know you by your values, which are expressed not by what you say so much as by what you do, how you think and speak, where and with whom you spend your time. Your values express the core of your true self. To live a congruent life is to live in alignment with your values.

When you lose sight of or ignore your values, an important part of you becomes obscured, and it is very easy to take a wrong turn and make unwise, unproductive choices. Like driving a car in dense fog, you can't clearly see what's ahead, and you could likely steer your car in the wrong direction or, even worse, steer off the road altogether. When this happens, you are out of alignment; you are divided, separated from your true self, your true voice. From a spiritual perspective, you are out of spiritual attunement. From an ecological perspective, some indigenous cultures would say that you are out of grace, out of order at all levels—personal, environmental, world, and spiritual.

EXERCISES

Set aside time when you won't have any distractions, and remember to use your notebook or journal for your notes.

- Make a list of people with whom you can be yourself. This means that as you speak with these people, you do not change yourself in any way; you are just as you truly know yourself to be.
- Make another list of people with whom you edit yourself. This means that you change your speech and your body language,

and to hide your anxiety or nervousness perhaps you laugh (or you don't or can't). Choose one person on your list and describe three or four ways that you behave differently in his or her presence. Call your list "Red Flags" and use it to learn about yourself, what you do, and how you act when you're not congruent. When you learn to recognize your flags, you can then take the creative action to replace your "Red Flag" behavior with a different behavior that is more like your usual, congruent self.

• Identify a symbol, metaphor, or image of integrity that is important in your life. Find or draw a picture of it and tape or glue it in your notebook or journal. List four qualities that signify its integrity. Write about it so that you can surface and explore the obvious and less obvious aspects of integrity. For example, one of my clients chose a mountain as his metaphor for integrity. He chose a specific mountain, Mount Rainier, and found a picture of it in a magazine. He listed these four qualities about the mountain that signified integrity to him:

  • Its beauty
  • Its awe-inspiring nature
  • Its great age
  • Its commanding presence

Here's an excerpt of what he wrote:

> I live on a dairy farm, just north of Olympia, Washington. This is an area of the Pacific Northwest where I can enjoy the majestic beauty of Mount Rainier. Its snow-covered dome looks so awesome against the blue sky. At over 14,400 feet, Mount Rainier towers above everything else for miles around. On clear days, you can see it from 100 miles away from any direction. When I can't see it because it's raining or is hidden behind the clouds, I can still feel its presence.
>
> The many faces and names of Mount Rainier help me understand the meaning of integrity. The mountain is true to itself. It is what it is at all times. A mountain. If a mountain can know itself, Mount Rainier does. This mountain does not long to be a

sand dune or an oyster. Mount Rainier is wholly and fully a glacier-covered mound of volcanic rock.

The locals call Mount Rainier "The Mountain." The native peoples who lived here before white settlers came called it Mount Tahoma. This ancient mountain reminds me of what it means to wear your soul on the outside, so I call it "My Father's Place." When I see Mount Rainier, I think of my dad. Strong. A man of few words. A commanding presence. Some days, you can see the lower two-thirds but not the top of the mountain. The top of it is covered by clouds. That's almost one mile of clouds! That's why locals also call Mount Rainier "The Weather Maker."

Integrity and Wholeness

The words *integrity, integer,* and *integral* share a common heritage; they all refer to a sense of wholeness, of being intact and complete. All too often, we associate this sense of wholeness with perfection. Not so. Integrity does not mean perfection. It does, however, include the ideal of perfection—not as a destination, but rather as something we strive toward in our journey toward wholeness. In that journey, we gain insight by learning more of what we need to know about ourselves to become fully human. This facet of integrity reminds me of sermons from my childhood in which the minister would exhort the congregation to remember that God was not done with us yet, that in fact our life is the crucible for our perpetual refining and perfecting—every day, every hour, every moment.

Because you are a work in progress, integrity calls you not only to be honest, truthful, and congruent, but also to lifelong intellectual and spiritual learning. This facet of integrity also requires the work of forgiveness—for yourself and others. Without forgiveness, we carry the time-worn, burdensome baggage from our past. Forgiveness frees us to focus on the present and the future.

Integrity means embracing and honoring all of your facets—acknowledging your beauty and brilliance as well as those aspects that you would rather keep hidden from view. As Marianne Williamson so splendidly expresses, "We are born to manifest the glory of God that is within us. . . . When we let our own light shine, we unconsciously give other people permission to do the same. As we are liberated from our own fear, our presence automatically liberates others." When you embrace and honor all facets of yourself, you serve as a mirror for others, a mirror in which they might catch a glimpse of their own beauty and magnificence, of what they might aspire to become.

Conversely, you also serve as a mirror for those aspects of yourself that psychologists call our shadow. According to the pioneering work of Carl Jung and others, our shadow consists of any aspect of ourselves that is cast off or unclaimed. Our shadow has two faces, one positive and the other negative. The positive face of our shadow consists of aspects of our signature presence that are deemed desirable, such as what Williamson describes as our beauty and brilliance. But because we haven't claimed or integrated these aspects of our nature, we keep them at bay or hidden from our conscious awareness. The negative face of our shadow consists of those dimensions of ourselves that we consider undesirable, flawed, defective, and unworthy, facets that we judge harshly.

Wholeness is the aspect of integrity that says, "I acknowledge all aspects of my nature, those aspects that I fully claim as well as *both* faces of my shadow, the positive and negative, which until now I've kept at arm's length." Perhaps at one time you were too scared, hurt, or intimidated by certain parts of your nature. Now you are ready to face these aspects, so that you can begin to integrate them into your whole self. Claiming and embracing all aspects of your signature presence, including your shadow, is your response to the invitation to wear your soul on the outside. The Sacred Promise of integrity, along with creative action and the other promises, are resources for your journey.

In our Western culture, integrity is most often perceived from an individualistic perspective. From this perspective, integrity is fundamentally about wholeness, and emanates from one source and one source only—from being true to yourself, fully yourself, and congruent with your values, for this is how you were designed. The challenge then is to integrate all of these aspects of yourself to return to your original state of wholeness.

Integrity as it relates to the collective is also fundamentally about wholeness. The collective in this sense consists of the whole of the "world community." Depending on the context, this means the world as you view it—for example, the "world" of your family, neighborhood, city, state, country, or continent. This view of integrity says, "My highest concern is for the whole rather than the individual parts. Rather than isolating individuals, cultures, nations, and so on, I care about the interdependence and interconnection of all parts." Maintaining this holistic perspective is among the crucial qualities that distinguished Lincoln's presidency during his long journey to keep the Union from disintegrating into split-off factions.

This view of the whole also says, "I appreciate diversity, for it is essential to all things." This view reveals our shared humanity across gender, generations, cultures, races, ethnicities, and worldviews, allows us to recognize our web of interconnectedness and interdependence, and invites us into the spaciousness of an *ecological* (from the Greek *oikos*, "house") sensibility. An ecological sensibility compels us to take special care of our many-roomed house, the rooms consisting of our personal bodies, our life-sustaining environment, the world body, and the spiritual body that connects us to ourselves, to one another, and to God.

EXERCISES

Set aside time when you won't have any distractions, and remember to use your notebook or journal for your notes.

- In your notebook or journal, draw a picture of your favorite tree. Make a list of what makes it whole, or complete. For example, "My tree has roots, a trunk, healthy branches, and leaves. In the spring, it has white flowers, and by summer it's filled with bright green apples." Now, on your drawing cross out one or two parts of your tree. Is it the same with parts of it missing? What's different about it? Does it matter? Why?
- What parts of you are missing, muted, or shut down? For example, if you were told as a child that you couldn't carry a tune, and you still believe it without having ever questioned it, you'd say that this part of you is muted, held back, or perhaps missing altogether.

(*Continued*)

- In your notebook or journal, draw two heart shapes. (You can also create two heart-shaped cutouts and tape or glue them into your notebook or journal.) Think about all the negative comments that have been said about you, your creativity, or your creative expression. For example, "You must have a tin ear. Every time you open your mouth to sing, my ears hurt. Go to the back of the choir, so no one will ever hear you." For each negative comment or word of disapproval, put a slash mark on one of your hearts.

- Now recall all of the positive things that have been said or that you could say about you, your creativity, or your creative expression. For example, "I love the sound of my voice. It's clear and pure. I have the voice of an angel." For each positive comment or word of praise, draw a star on your other heart.

- Now look at the two hearts and list all the comments or words that take away from your sense of wholeness. Make another list of all the comments or words that add to your sense of wholeness. Copy the second list onto another sheet of paper, and carry it with you to look at when you need a little boost. The creative actions of acknowledging what detracts from and what contributes to your wholeness move you toward integration.

- Is there a person in your life you would like to forgive? If so, write the person's name and what you would like to forgive on a slip of paper. Keep the paper in your notebook or journal until your negative feelings about that person are gone, totally released. When we forgive ourselves and others, we no longer need to carry baggage from our past. Forgiveness is a creative action that frees up our energy for the present and the future.

WAKE-UP CALL

At the heart of it all, our life's journey is all about our return to wholeness, one of the most exciting yet arduous assignments of being human. Sometimes we are pulled away from our calling through no fault of our own. At other times, as my friend Regina discovered, we are the sole culprit in sidestepping our calling. After starting out on the fast-track, Regina quickly made a name for herself as a top-notch computer engineer. When her clients hit a snag in their work, they called her for help. She enjoyed the thrill of solving complex computer problems, especially those that seemed to elude others. No problem seemed too difficult or time-consuming for her to tackle. In fact, problem solving was the aspect of engineering Regina loved the most.

Almost ten years ago, she woke up suddenly in the middle of the night in her hotel room in Houston, Texas, and wondered aloud, "What on earth am I doing in this job? Do I really want to be working as a computer engineer twenty years from now?"

> I don't recall why I woke up. Perhaps I'd been dreaming. . . .
> I remember feeling as if someone had called my name and startled me awake. I sat up in bed and for a few moments just stared at the glowing display on the alarm clock. For the first time in years, I began to think about my work, which I enjoyed. New people to meet, new places to travel, and new problems to solve.

On this particular sleepless night, Regina began to think about her future in earnest. At thirty-three, she was still happily single. Though she planned to get married and have several children of her own someday, Regina was in no hurry either to marry or start a family. Because her work schedule often demanded long hours and extended periods of travel, adoption and foster care were also out of the question. As she thought about how much she loved children, she let her mind wander: "Maybe I can figure out how I can include children in some aspect of my work. I wonder if my company has a program where I can mentor children in math." Her thoughts drifted back to her first year of college, when she was still in a pre-med program. Back then she really wanted to be a doctor. Medicine. This was her first love. Not engineering or computers.

> As an undergraduate, I switched majors from pre-med to engineering, because I was a bit squeamish about blood and I was afraid to work on cadavers, which was part of the deal if you wanted to be a doctor.
>
> When I think about spending the next twenty-five or maybe thirty years working, I want to wake up every day not just excited about my work, I also want to know that I'm making a difference in someone else's life.

Even before her long night of soul searching, Regina's inner voice had called her to return to medicine, her first love. At this stage in her life, she could now imagine herself as a doctor. Maybe she could work in an area that would allow her to use her knowledge of computing and engineering. Medical research, perhaps. No, too removed. She loved being around people and couldn't envision her future without children in it. Even in her free time, she volunteered as a tutor in the schools. Perhaps she'd become a pediatrician. Regina thought about the long road ahead of her. She'd have to brush up on her science and math to prepare for medical school entrance exams, commit to going to school for four years plus a three-year residency, and confront her fear of working with cadavers. As she reset the alarm, she said to herself, "I am ready for the challenge."

The next day, Regina called her parents from her hotel room and asked if she could move in with them for a couple of years so she could save as much of her salary as possible to pay for medical school. They agreed. For the next two years, she continued to work as a computer engineer by day. At night, she attended community college to brush up on math and science in preparation for medical school. As she did, she formed a vision of her future practice.

> I want to be the kind of doctor that I had when I was growing up . . .
> the kind who served everyone equally whether or not they could
> pay . . . who spent time with you and really cared about you as a
> whole person, not just your sickness or injury. I love being around
> kids, and I want to help them become the best they can be.

Regina applied and was admitted to several medical schools. She wanted to be close to her family, so she chose a school about an hour's drive away. Six years after that night in her Houston hotel room, Regina graduated near the top of her class. Her entire family attended her graduation to celebrate with her as she received her M.D. degree.

Today, Regina runs a thriving pediatric practice. She is known for her generosity, compassion, and devotion to her patients and their families. Parents appreciate her problem-solving skills, which saves them costly and unnecessary trips to the hospital. Most important, Regina is fired up about her practice and can't wait to go to work each day. She knows from her young patients, who call her "Dr. Reggi," and their families that she is making a difference in their lives. At home, some of the youngsters "play doctor." And in their imaginative world of play where you can do or be anything or anyone, they pretend their name is Dr. Reggi.

As a pre-med student primed to fulfill her childhood dream of becoming a doctor, Regina entered college on track with her calling. She was also on track with two aspects of integrity, being true to herself and congruent with her values. However, as an engineer, though she managed to maintain her overarching goal of helping others, following another career path cost Regina her sense of congruence, chipping away at her wholeness.

As Regina discovered, sometimes you must find out what you want by experiencing what you don't want, echoing Carl Jung when he says that "The right way to wholeness is through fitful starts and wrong turnings." Jung also wisely counsels that "only that which is truly one's self has the power to heal," the power to restore you to wellness and wholeness. And both evoke the energies of creativity, wonder, joy, awe, and rapture, reminding us once again of Williamson's words that we are born to manifest God's glory, the glory that is within each of us. When we honor our integrity, strive to become all that God intended us to be, and wear our souls on the outside, we enchant, illuminate, and inspire others. Just ask Dr. Reggi.

AFFIRMATIONS: I'M DOING IT!

- I follow my own internal compass.
- I can be myself with my coworkers.
- I communicate openly and honestly with my spouse or significant other.
- I stay connected to others even when we disagree with one another.
- I am comfortable with openly expressing my thoughts, opinions, and feelings.
- I am congruent in what I believe and what I do.

(*Continued*)

- Others see me as congruent; they see that "I walk my talk."
- I am committed to expressing my signature presence.
- I can speak my truth and preserve relationships with family, friends, and coworkers and within my community.
- I am committed to expressing my brilliance and magnificence and not hiding any parts of myself.

By choosing integrity, I become more whole, but wholeness does not mean perfection. It means becoming more real by acknowledging the whole of who I am.
PARKER J. PALMER

CHAPTER 9

Creative Action—Manifestation and Fulfillment

> *My hope is to expand the definition of creativity so that more of us—all of us—can begin to perceive ourselves as creators, to pay attention to what rises up from our depths in response to our daily experiences, and to do something with it.*
> JAN PHILLIPS

IT'S SELDOM EASY TO JUMP SHIP from a job in corporate America and set sail at the helm of your own successful enterprise. But that's exactly what Chris McIntyre and Jeff Brown did. Former executives in the telecommunications industry, Chris and Jeff founded and now, along with a couple of other executives, run the world's largest motorcycle rental and touring company, Eagle Rider.

Founded in 1992, Eagle Rider stocks Harley-Davidsons of all types and offers their adventure-seeking customers an opportunity of a lifetime—the chance to live an American fantasy, the chance to unleash their inner Easy Rider. To ensure that customers will be properly outfitted to ride their Harley-Davidson dream machines, they can shop in Eagle Rider stores for "rebel wear," including caps, shirts, bandannas, and leather jackets.

Eagle Rider's slogan couldn't be more fitting: "We rent dreams." How else would you have the chance to leave the busyness and responsibilities of your regular world, and ride out of town on a Harley to experience the exhilaration of fresh air streaming around you, the open road, and the vacation of a lifetime—all without the expense and hassle of ownership and maintenance?

Motorcycle enthusiasts since boyhood, Chris and Jeff launched Eagle Rider to fill a void in the market, which they stumbled on when they wanted to rent bikes for a European tour they'd envisioned as part of their sabbaticals. When they began to look for Harley rental companies, they found none—either in Europe or the United States. That market void gave birth to a new idea. Today, Eagle Rider has offices in more than several dozen cities across the United States, and in Europe, Australia, Mexico, and Central America. In addition to Harleys, they also rent BMW and Honda bikes, as well as personal watercraft, snowmobile, and all-terrain vehicles. The company also offers guided tours for solo or group riders. Ranging from several days to two weeks and longer, Eagle Rider tours boast titles befitting Hollywood, such as "Rocky Mountain High," "California Dreamin'," "Kilts and Bagpipes," and "Biker's Paradise."

Chris and Jeff cherish the culture they have created at Eagle Rider—spirited, nimble, and passion-filled. They realize that passion is their "secret sauce" and know all too well that without passion to fuel and sustain you, "you can become dead men walking" as an entrepreneur or in corporate America. And without passion, you have a difficult time attracting customers and staff. Though they don't get away from the office as often as they'd like these days, Chris and Jeff are glad to be out of the snares of corporate life, expanding the business they've created, and making dreams come true for others.

CREATIVE ACTION AND CREATIVITY

Creative action is all about getting something done, which you already know how to do if you've gotten this far in your life and in this book. Creative action is a special way to mobilize your own and others' energy so you can act with *specific intention* to form, shape, make something happen, or bring forth something that would not otherwise come into being.

Creative action begins with a thought or idea of what you want to manifest, which you then turn into something tangible, such as a list, a note, a phone call, an interview, a blueprint, or a garden. All of these are creative actions that will lead to dozens or even hundreds of other creative actions. Eagle Rider began as an idea to fill a void in the marketplace. That single creative action opened the door for Chris and Jeff to connect to what had heart and meaning for them and put them on the road to realizing their deepest desires and dreams. The same can be true for you.

The Sacred Promise of creative action underscores your unique creativity, which is your birthright and an expression of your divinity. In contrast to creative action, which is all about doing, creativity is about both doing and being, with an emphasis on the latter. Creativity calls you to take the stance of a creator and actually be a creator. When you embody this stance, everything that you are and do takes on an entirely different dimension and transcends the ordinary—that is, transcends the stifling assumption that creativity is "out there" rather than inside you.

For some of you, embracing and embodying a creative stance means giving yourself permission to be creative, not comparing yourself to others, and taking responsibility for your creativity. Both creative action and creativity are about creative equanimity, which simply means that we are all equally creative. The relevant question is not "Am I creative?" It is "How will I use my creativity to make a positive difference in my own and someone else's life?"

As you work through the *Questions for Reflection,* think creatively about your calling that you discovered and identified in Chapter Two. Now consider your calling as something that you want to manifest, something that you want to make concrete and tangible with creative action so that if you could reach out and touch it, you'd say, "Yes, this is it! This is my first step toward my calling—my new career, volunteering in my community, my life after retirement."

QUESTIONS FOR REFLECTION

Set aside time when you won't have any distractions, and remember to use your notebook or journal for your notes.

• What does or could creative action mean to you?

- What is or could be the rhythm, or presence, of creative action in your life?
- What does or could creativity mean to you?
- What is or could be the rhythm, or presence, of creativity in your life?
- Who are the three women and three men you most admire? Jot down their names and why you admire them. Choose one woman and one man from your list and describe one of their significant accomplishments. How did creative action and creativity play a part in their accomplishments?

Although the Sacred Promise of creative action stands alone, it is also an essential aspect of all the other promises. Think of creative action as the gas pedal in your car. Without creative action, your passionate intention, signature presence, and all the other Sacred Promises have no fuel. If you take your foot off the gas pedal, the car stops.

Creative action offers you the power of manifestation and fulfillment. Manifestation is a process that consists of the concrete expression, demonstration, implementation, and completion of what you want to create. An ongoing process, manifestation requires creative action *and* follow through, and it unfolds over time until whatever you start is completed. Fulfillment is the satisfaction of experiencing and completing whatever it is you want to manifest—the sense of contentment after painting your bedroom, the heart-warming joy of mending a friendship, the satisfaction of successfully launching a new business. Fulfillment can also unfold during the process of manifestation. Be sure to celebrate your accomplishments along the way toward manifestation. To take a small or big step toward manifesting and fulfilling your dreams, creative action requires **clarity**, **courage**, **conviction**, and **commitment**.

Clarity

Each of us has an open invitation to ask for and pursue what we want to manifest. To ask for what you *truly* want, begin with a clear, specific intention. To gain clarity, state your intention aloud: "I want to learn to paint." This is a good beginning, but it lacks specificity, which you can achieve by asking yourself, "What type of painting do I want to learn about? Do I want to paint with water-colors, acrylics, oils?" When you're satisfied with the level of specificity, ask for confirmation of your intention by tuning into and listening to your powerful inner voice, and have faith that what you seek will be given to you and manifested through you.

Many years ago, Becca and I worked for the same small, close-knit company. When she took a position at another company, we lost touch until a few years ago when we were once again consulting for the same organization. One day over coffee Becca confided that for years she had been searching for her calling, her deepest purpose in life. Now in her mid-forties, she is delighted that she has discovered it.

> I always thought I'd join some group that protested the war or worked to save the environment, and there I would figure out how I was going to save the planet. That never happened, and for many years I felt like a failure. But now as I get older, I realize that I am not made to be a speaker—either public speaking or debating—or even door-to-door grassroots speaking. I could push myself to do that, but I am happiest when I am alone.
>
> The Sacred Promises have helped me understand some of the questions I've been asking since I was in my teens: What am I here for? What is my purpose? I've always enjoyed working with my hands. I really love making pottery, but I gave that up years ago. More and more, I feel pulled to do my pottery again.

During the next several months, as Becca listened to the inner voice that kept tugging at her, pulling her to devote herself to making pots, she asked herself, "What kinds of pots do I want to make? Who am I making them for? What is my specific intention in making pots?" You may notice that these are the same kinds of questions, worded differently, that you have been asked to consider throughout the chapters of this book. *What matters to me? What do I stand for? What do I want to create and for whom?* As Becca reflected on these questions, she gradually received the clarity she was seeking.

> I love making pots because it brings me great joy and satisfaction, and I want to pour my love and joy into my pots and share it with others. I now realize that making pots is, in large part, my spirituality.

Courage

Courageous seeking, asking, and listening strengthens your creativity. Each of these creative actions builds your creative muscle. Courage means communicating your clear, specific intention from your heart and listening with your heart, which means to listen from within. It also helps to listen with childlike ears and see with the eyes of a child. Get curious and playful. Indulge yourself in wonder. Ask yourself, "How would this person or situation sound or look through the eyes of my five- or six-year-old self?" By assuming this perspective, you open yourself to discovery, learning, and beneficial surprise.

Courage also means acting on your intention from your heart. When you act from your heart, intending to be of service, courage can become as natural as breathing. Becca sought her calling, listened with her heart for the response, and acted on what she wanted to create. Through these and many other creative actions, Becca brought forth her signature presence, expressing her creativity through making pottery.

> I no longer wonder about my purpose in life. I am now certain that pottery is my calling. I am just blown away by how much satisfaction I get from it. I get to make things that others can use and that inspire them as well. How cool is that?

Conviction

When you act with clarity, courage, and conviction, you generate the necessary momentum to set purposeful goals and take positive steps toward manifesting what you want to create. Conviction says, "This is what I care about so deeply that I must do it. I will take the creative actions needed to make my vision a reality." Without conviction, your vision will remain a vision—an ingenious potentiality, perhaps, but one that will ultimately wither and not bear fruit.

When your vision of what you want to manifest is clear and you act on it with courage and conviction, like Becca, you accept the dare to wear your soul on the outside. You live into and embody the vision that you seek.

> As I work the clay and mix the glazes for my pots, I feel like I'm putting a piece of myself in them. Each plate and cup has its own story and its own soul, and each piece is connected to my spirit.
>
> Other people seem to enjoy my pottery. When I tell them about pouring my values of spiritual, intentional living into my pieces, they seem to appreciate and resonate with that.

Commitment

When you act with clarity, courage, conviction, and commitment, you will manifest your vision. An essential dimension of creative action, commitment proclaims, "In addition to *saying* I will act, I am now *doing* something about it. I am committed to following through on my idea. I am committed to taking the creative actions necessary to turn my idea into a painting, a composition, a studio or office near my home."

You are probably already accomplished in initiating and generating ideas, using "to do" lists or brainstorming. To transform your ideas into tangible, meaningful results, you must act. An action plan will help you translate your ideas into clear, specific goals—but to move from plan to reality, you need energy, focus, and commitment. With commitment or follow-through, you will turn your idea into a meaningful conversation, a succulent casserole, a talking circle for teens, or a new playhouse for your son's day care center. You will turn your good intentions into helping your neighbor by shoveling her snow or driving her to the clinic. Becca's commitment to her vision became manifest in her beautiful pottery.

> In the process of making pots, I am creating vessels that are both beautiful and useful. I'm also being of service to others. I understand now that my pots are my children. They are my legacy. When a customer looks at and holds a pitcher or vase that I made, they are literally holding the outpouring of my heart and hands, my "voice," as you call it, in the palm of their hands.

Creative action and creativity move you beyond thinking and saying to manifestation and fulfillment. By embracing her creativity and through her thoughtful creative actions—seeking clarity and acting with courage, conviction, and commitment—Becca manifested what she wanted in her work and lifestyle. She is living her legacy. Just like Becca, you can embody a creative stance as your way of being and take positive, forward-moving actions daily in the direction of what you want to manifest so that you, too, can live your legacy now.

As you complete the next set of *Exercises,* set a passionate intention for yourself and for others and ask yourself, "What passionate intention is waiting to be fulfilled through me?"

EXERCISES

Set aside time when you won't have any distractions, and remember to use your notebook or journal for your notes.

- In your notebook or journal, draw a stick figure of yourself doing something for someone else. Choose anything at all that fits for you—house-sitting, making a meal for a sick neighbor, volunteering at a pet shelter. All of these activities are forms of creative action.
- If you have an idea but are not quite clear about what you want to manifest, jot down whatever is clear to you now. For the next fourteen days, take the creative action of coming back to this exercise at least once a day and making a note about whatever comes through for you.
- Find a quotation or short poem that captures the essence of creativity. Write it down in your notebook or journal. Memorize the quotation or poem.
- Think of three or four activities from your childhood that light up your face and bring you absolute joy—blowing bubbles, finger painting, making funny faces. Choose one activity and do it each day for a week to kick-start or celebrate your creativity.

OVERCOME BLOCKS TO CREATIVE ACTION AND CREATIVITY

Prolific inventor Thomas Edison said, "An idea is something that won't work unless you do." The same holds true for creative action and creativity. If you have an idea or vision of what you want, nothing will happen to move you toward it unless you take some form of creative action. You must put your foot on the gas pedal.

Many things can hold you back or get in the way of your taking that step of faith, counting your blessings, creating a meaningful personal vision, or staying on track with what you want to achieve. The chief blocks to creative action and creativity are **your inner critic**, **insecurity**, **procrastination**, **speed**, and **focus**. To deal effectively with and overcome any of these blocks, think of them as opportunities for learning and growth. Ask yourself:

- What can I learn from this person or circumstance?
- What do I need to unlearn or let go of to manifest what I want to create?
- How are my blocks keeping me from seeing or knowing what I need to see or know?

Your Inner Critic

Your inner critic may be a single voice or multiple voices. Most often these voices emanate from your past, yet you carry them with you as though they are actually present. Your inner critic might be the voice of your well-meaning parent, sibling, teacher, friend—anyone who at some point in your life discouraged, criticized, or said something that you construed as hurtful. Regardless of that person's true intention, you internalized his or her comments or deeds as a critical, judgmental voice.

Steve is a corporate attorney for a large insurance company. When he explored the Sacred Promises during a recent workshop, he recognized that his inner critic's voice was drowning out his own voice, squelching his desire to express himself through his real passion, photography.

> My dad was an attorney for a prominent law firm. His father was an attorney at the same firm. Though my dad never said I had to

follow in his footsteps, he made it very clear that he wasn't going to pay for me to go to college unless I studied pre-law. He might as well have said, "Don't waste your time and talent on anything else."

You can recognize your inner critic by what he or she says. All variations on the same theme, the familiar scripts include: "Oh, you can't do *that*. No one in our family has ever done that before." "You're much too old" (or too young, inexperienced, talented, smart, awkward, tall, short). "Who do you think you are?" "You're wasting your time. That will never work." "Do as I say, or else . . ." You probably have your own variations as well.

Your goal is to have compassion for and to triumph over your chorus of critical voices. You do this by turning down the volume on their disapproving advice while turning up the volume on your own voice, which you can do by focusing on your vision, passionate intention, and goals. When your chorus of critics insists on airtime, acknowledge them: "Oh, hi there. It's you again. Thanks for caring enough to stop by. I know you mean well, but I'm going to do what's best for me." Then purposefully move on in the direction of *your* vision.

On the journey to wearing your soul on the outside, you must be in the driver's seat. The ultimate goal is to acknowledge your critical "sidekicks"—and then kindly usher them away from the driver's seat and out of the car. Drive away, and don't look back. As they disappear from view in your rearview mirror you can wave goodbye. If this sounds a bit harsh, just remember that this is *your* life and this creative action puts you in the driver's seat where you belong.

Insecurity

If your inner critic sounds like your own voice, insecurity may be at work. In our culture, because we are often intimidated by our own creativity, it is easy to be overcome by insecurity, which can take many forms. You can be afraid of your own brilliance and magnificence, of being judged and not fitting in or belonging, of not having enough knowledge, skill, time, experience, and so on. You can also be insecure about not *being* enough, as though you are inadequate, insufficient, or inferior in some way.

The antidote to insecurity and the accompanying doubt, anxiety, and fear is what Rollo May calls the "courage to create." In his seminal book *The Courage to Create*, May says that this is "the most important kind of courage of all." He explains that "creative courage is the discovering of new forms, new symbols, new patterns." I would add that creative courage summons you to move boldly through your insecurity and discover new ways of being so that you can express what can only come through you. As my soccer coach used to say, "You can't play the game sitting on the sidelines." Similarly, you cannot live passionately and joyously by "sitting it out" or by merely thinking about it. What new project, relationship, or volunteer opportunity is waiting for you?

May also recognizes that "every profession can and does require some creative courage." As twenty-first-century citizens living in a vast and complex global village, not only do our professions require some form of creative courage, most aspects of daily living require it as well. In his *Book of Awakening*, Mark Nepo talks about "the paradox that underscores all courage: that leaning into what is gripping us will allow us to work our way free." In other words, one way out of insecurity is through it. I see the success of this leaning in to insecurity time and again in my work with clients, students, and in my own life. Another way out is "service first," which one of my students summed up this way: "When you put service to others ahead of your own doubts and fears, your own lack of confidence or insecurity becomes less important and often disappears altogether."

Procrastination

Procrastination means that you are giving more attention to non-urgent or less important concerns than to what's important to you. If you find yourself making excuses, deferring, or delaying taking creative action toward your vision, then you are probably procrastinating. Procrastination assumes many guises: shopping, cleaning, eating, surfing the Internet, idle conversation, watching too much television. Even doing those things that are good for us, such as exercise or calling friends, can be a form of procrastination, *if* the activity diverts your attention away from the main thing.

When I was writing my first children's book, I consulted with my friend Jeanie, author of a number of successful children's books. I wanted to understand the nuances of writing for children and to ensure that my work was historically accurate. Knowing my penchant for research, Jeanie wisely counseled, "If you're spending far more time and energy on research than actually writing, then you're probably procrastinating." She was right. Though it was important to be historically accurate, at times my research was a delaying tactic, an unnecessary diversion from my chief goal, which was to write my book.

Speed

Like procrastination, moving too quickly can be the antithesis of creative action and creativity. The Sacred Promise of creative action insists that you slow down in order to focus and direct your passionate intention, get clarity about what you want to create and for whom, and have a plan of action. During a recent visit to my dentist's office, I overheard a woman in the waiting area talking to her friend about her home remodel. She described the project in great detail, clearly frustrated that the work was taking far longer than she anticipated. Her friend, who hadn't uttered a word until this moment, kindly asked, "Do you want your home done well, or do you want it done soon?" A good question for all of us.

Renowned for his phenomenal speed and ability in the long jump, Jesse Owens was almost assured of victory at the Berlin Olympic Games of 1936. In *The Complete Book of the Olympics,* historian and sports authority David Wallechinsky explains that in the prior year, Owens had jumped a distance of well over twenty-six feet, setting a record that would remain unbroken for a quarter of a century. Even so, "Owens felt nervous. He was acutely aware of the Nazis' desire to prove 'Aryan superiority,' especially over blacks."

Because of his speed, Owens had inadvertently fouled on his first two leaps in the qualifying rounds. With only one attempt remaining, one of his competitors approached him, a tall, blond, blue-eyed German who introduced himself as Luz Long. Referring to his two jumps, Long said, "You should be able to qualify with your eyes closed!" Wallechinsky tells us that for the next few moments the black son of a sharecropper and the white model of Nazi manhood chatted. Then Long made a suggestion. Since the qualifying distance was only 23 feet, 5½ inches, why not make a mark several inches before the takeoff board and jump from there, just to play it safe? Owens did and qualified easily.

By setting a mark before the takeoff board, Owens's phenomenal speed would work for him rather than against him as it presumably did on his previous qualifying jumps.

In the finals Owens set an Olympic record and earned the second of four golds. The first person to congratulate him was Luz Long—in full view of Adolf Hitler.

Though they never saw one another again, Owens later wrote, "You could melt down all the medals and cups I have, and they wouldn't be plating on the 24-karat friendship I felt for Luz Long." Owens's and Long's sportsmanlike behavior demonstrates that creative action can emerge from your own efforts or from the efforts of others who act on your behalf, and it also highlights the importance of compassion in the creative process—for yourself and for others.

Focus

Years ago an artist friend taught me this simple yet powerful way to shift your awareness from being blocked, which freezes your energy, to being unblocked, which frees up your energy and unleashes your creativity. To make the shift, you must first bring to your consciousness that you are stuck or blocked. You can say something as simple as "Oh, I'm stuck." Then, without being critical or judgmental of yourself, simply acknowledge your current reality: "I'm busy doing *this* (whatever it is you're doing), which is distracting me from getting on with *that* (whatever it is you want to manifest)." Your acknowledgment of what is so ("Oh, I'm stuck") will shift your awareness and bring you into the present where you can make the productive choice to redirect your focus from *this* (for example, procrastinating or listening to your inner critic) to *that,* focusing your energy on and taking a creative action toward what you want to achieve.

To be at your creative best requires passionate intention and devotion to what you want to achieve. To effectively deal with any of the blocks to creative action and creativity, remember to think of them as opportunities for learning and growth. As you prepare for the next set of *Exercises,* ask yourself the questions I asked you to consider earlier in this chapter: "What can I learn from this person or circumstance?" "What do I need to unlearn or let go of to manifest what I want to create?" and "How are my blocks keeping me from seeing or knowing what I need to see or know?"

EXERCISES

Set aside time when you won't have any distractions, and remember to use your notebook or journal for your notes.

- Make a list of affirmations for creative action and creativity in your journal or notebook. You can use the affirmations below as a model for yours or use them as some of your own.

  - I recognize that being creative is my birthright.
  - I choose to take a creative stance, not a reactive one.
  - I journal regularly.
  - When things don't go as planned, I adjust and adapt.
  - I am not waiting for permission to pursue what I want to manifest.
  - I demonstrate clarity, courage, conviction, and commitment by taking positive steps toward my goals.
  - I imagine possibilities when others see obstacles and road blocks.
  - I see mistakes and failure as necessary aspects of the creative process.
  - I understand the connection of creative action to each of the other Sacred Promises.

- Create a "Bowl of Compassion" for your inner critic, your chorus of critical voices. For the next month, whenever one of your critics or chorus members "shows up," write a word or phrase of compassion to him or her and put it in your bowl. Doing this exercise will ease you into the process of letting go of your inner critic so that you can free up your valuable energy for your vision that can only come through your life force.

- Review the following summary of common blocks to creative action and creativity and how to overcome them. In your journal or notebook, for each block add two or three strategies that you can use to effectively overcome them.

Common Blocks	Do This
Inner critic	Be compassionate with yourself and your inner critic as you turn up the volume on your own inner voice and turn down the volume on your inner critic's voice.
Insecurity	Move through your insecurity to discover new ways of being. Summon the courage to create.
Procrastination	Redirect your focus from non-urgent concerns to your passionate intention, so that you can take the creative action necessary for what you want to achieve.
Speed	Slow down. Set your intention. Get clear about what you want to create. Have a plan of action.
Focus	Shift your focus from being stuck to unstuck. Keep it simple. Take a creative action by choosing a productive next step.

The Sacred Promise of creative action offers you the power of manifestation and fulfillment. It affirms creativity as your birthright and addresses the question "How will I use my creativity to make a positive difference in my own and someone else's life?" Creative action provides the resources of clarity, courage, conviction, and commitment as well as resources to support you in effectively dealing with and overcoming common blocks. In your journey toward manifestation and fulfillment, creative action calls you to recognize the value of your own resourcefulness and invites you to remember the powerful resources of passionate intention, compassion, and service.

> *I don't know what your destiny will be, but one thing I know: the only ones among you who will be truly happy are those who have sought and found how to serve.*
> ALBERT SCHWEITZER

CHAPTER 10

Legacy—Service and Stewardship

One of the most calming and powerful actions you can do to intervene in a stormy world is to stand up and show your soul. Soul on deck shines like gold in dark times. . . . Struggling souls catch light from other souls who are fully lit and willing to show it.
CLARISSA PINKOLA ESTES

WHEN I WAS A LITTLE GIRL, I thought I lived in an all-black town. Segregation ensured that we kept to ourselves. Too young to understand the meaning of the word *segregation,* I simply felt as if we lived in our very own town. Although I didn't know the meaning of the word, I certainly felt its impact. I knew it by the tightness in my stomach whenever I went into a shop in the "other town" with my parents and they politely addressed the white shopkeepers as Mr. or Mrs. So-and-So, yet the shopkeepers called my parents by their first names.

From my earliest experiences of segregation, I detested everything about it. Outraged that all the freedoms I experienced at home with my family were denied me when we were among whites, I resolved to stand up for myself and for my rights and to speak out against injustice. Even as a youngster, I knew that I wanted to make it impossible for anyone to treat my parents, my sisters, me, or anyone else differently because of the color of our skin. Little did I know that the scaffold of my legacy was already under construction.

KEEP YOUR EYES ON THE PRIZE

With the blessing of hindsight on my part and foresight on yours, you can be intentional about your legacy. Inside every human being is a glorious world longing to be born. Your responsibility is to be a midwife, so to speak—to heat the water and bring in the towels—to help give birth to these magnificent new worlds. Once birthed, your role is to be of service as steward, caretaker, and caregiver—for our children, our workplaces, our communities, our civic institutions, and our earth. Service is the essence of the Sacred Promise of legacy.

Legacy compels you to heed your own calling and passion, to keep your creative fires burning so that you will be able to pass the flame on to others. In this sense, you are obliged to serve as both midwife and torchbearer, to humbly aid in the birth of new ideas, projects, compositions, inventions, schools, legislation, or other creations, as well as to faithfully tend the hearth of your own calling.

In her essay "Standing Up for Children," Marion Wright Edelman, founder and president of the Children's Defense Fund, writes about legacy as our living testament to who and what matters. A tireless champion for children, Edelman says, "The great events of this world are not battles and elections and earthquakes and thunderbolts. The great events are babies, for each child comes with the message that God is not yet discouraged with humanity, but is still expecting goodwill to become incarnate in each human life."

If you envision your life as a relay race, and if the recipients of the baton are your children, and if the winner of the race can determine the future of humankind, don't you want your baton to be one of goodwill and love?

Your life *is* something of a relay race, and what you pass on is the precious baton of your values and beliefs, your principles and practices, your decisions and choices, the sum total of who you are. The baton that you pass on is your legacy, your spiritual inheritance, which is destined to have a lasting impact on the lives of your children, their children, and beyond. It is your responsibility, indeed it is your obligation, to keep your eyes on this, your most valued prize.

In our culture, most people believe that your legacy is something that occurs only after you die. Nothing could be further from the truth. While you *will* leave a legacy upon your death, your legacy can be better appreciated and understood as a process—living, organic, and always evolving. Your legacy is much more than something out there in the great beyond. Your legacy is always forming. Its materials include both who you are right now and who you are becoming. Like the currents of a mighty river, your legacy is always in motion, continuously flowing. You and your legacy are a work in progress. Indeed, your legacy is your magnum opus, your supreme and magnificent life's work.

As you review and answer the *Questions for Reflection,* think about the people who have made a favorable difference in your life.

QUESTIONS FOR REFLECTION

Set aside time when you won't have any distractions, and remember to use your notebook or journal for your notes.

- What does legacy mean to you?
- What is the rhythm, or presence, of legacy in your life?
- How do you want to be known and remembered?
- What choices do you make daily to live your legacy here and now?
- What do you believe in so deeply and passionately that you will make enormous sacrifices for it?

THE DANCE OF LIFE

As you discovered in Chapter Two, you have been summoned to become a person unique in all the world. Just as every snowflake and leaf is unique, so are you. No one else is like you or can contribute what you were specifically designed to contribute.

Dancing visionary and pioneer Martha Graham likens dancing to the art of living. Both require years of practice and development. In her autobiography *Blood Memory,* Graham points out that we "learn to dance by practicing dancing" and we "learn to live by practicing living." In dancing and in living, the principles are the same. Each is the performance of a dedicated, precise set of acts, physical or intellectual, from which comes the shape of achievement, the sense of one's being, the satisfaction of spirit.

For dancing and for living, we learn what we need to know through practice, which requires thousands of repetitions. To learn and master walking, talking, and feeding yourself requires several years of practice. You learned to walk by practicing the basics, first learning to crawl or scoot, then pushing and pulling into the vertical realm to grasp the eager and encouraging hands of your parents, or a table leg, chair, or anything else strong enough to give you the confidence to begin again after the inevitable triumph of gravity over your miniature yet ever aspiring body.

Practice is the act of doing something in some aspect of our lives over and over until the act becomes habit or instinct, so customary that it becomes integral in two ways—first, to your way of doing whatever you are practicing and then to your way of being, inextricably connecting what you do with who you are.

Dancers learn to dance by practicing the fundamentals of their craft over and over again until they can move on to intermediate and advanced levels; their training is designed to build, strengthen, shape, and hone their bodies' musculature, reflexes, and memory. Graham estimates that making a mature dancer takes about ten years. This span of a decade in the dancer's training is analogous to the formative years of your life when you learn the fundamental tasks and assignments of living—the basic arts of relationship, nourishment, mobility, and possibility.

As Graham reminds us, it is no small wonder that dance holds an ageless allure, for "it has been the symbol of the performance of living." In your life's journey—or your life's performance, if you will—some of the most important questions that you ask and grapple with may be questions about your legacy. Host these questions as you would a special guest in your home. Pay attention, but avoid hovering over them. In time, the questions will take up residence in your heart, and they will reveal their secrets to you. As you keep your eyes on the great prize of your life, they will become your teacher and guide.

The next set of *Exercises* is designed to give you a sense of what's really important to you and to celebrate yourself.

EXERCISES

Set aside time when you won't have any distractions, and remember to use your notebook or journal for your notes.

- Put on your favorite music. In your notebook or journal, list twenty activities or things that you positively love. Choose five that make you feel like you're on top of the world! Now, choose one that you can't live without.
- List five things you want to accomplish before you die. Choose one that you most want to do and circle it. In your notebook or journal, write a letter to your best friend explaining, in the present tense, what you have accomplished, as if you have reached your goal. Here's how such a letter might begin:

> Dear Leslie,
>   I'm writing this note with a huge smile on my face. I'm so excited to share my good news with you.

- Read the letter aloud to yourself each day for the next week. At the end of the week, celebrate yourself by doing something special—sleeping in late, eating breakfast in bed, taking a walk, enjoying your favorite specialty coffee or tea beverage, reading your favorite book.

One of the ways I have kept my eyes on the future is by sharing stories and poetry, time-honored ways to impart wisdom and to teach what might otherwise take months or years. My stories and poems have also helped me work through the pain and anger of my past. When shared with others, stories and poems offer a lifeline or a bridge, a beacon or a candle in someone else's life. You just never know when something will awaken in others that allows them to surface and share *their* stories. Poet Theodore Roethke expressed that we all "learn by going where [we] have to go."

A couple of years ago, I delivered a keynote for an International Women's Leadership Conference convened in Europe. The organizers invited me to speak about authentic leadership. They knew of my work in developing and coaching leaders and of my work as a storyteller and poet. I was one of the few speakers from the United States and was sensitive to an anti-American sentiment among some of the conference participants.

As I prepared my presentation, I contemplated how I might serve as an ambassador not only for authentic leadership but also as an instrument for reconciliation. I was reminded of Archbishop Tutu's invitational words—"God is waiting on us. He needs our help." Reflecting on them, I asked myself: During this particular conference, how might God need my help?

After my presentation, I knew the answer.

Instead of standing behind the podium, which was a considerable distance from the audience, I stepped downstage near the edge of the platform. Though I had prepared notes, I decided in the moment not to use them. I spoke extemporaneously, from my heart, telling stories from my life and sharing my own poems to illustrate key points. I did not talk about authentic leadership; I modeled it, showing my true self, using my true voice to illuminate the most essential aspects of leadership, aspects that in Western culture are too often ignored. I represented a mirror in which participants could see a glimpse of their own reflected light, their own possibility.

As I was speaking, I saw that many in the audience were on the edge of their seat—some literally. The room was charged with enthusiasm. I mean enthusiasm in the sense of its connection to *entheos*—inspired by the gods. The audience was at once excited and expectant for what they could become, for their own possibilities now that they were armed with this new, so easily received wisdom. When I concluded my presentation, I received a standing ovation. I mention this to emphasize that the audience received my keynote as a demonstration of daring to wear your soul on the outside! By speaking from my heart without my notes, I walked my talk, modeling a legacy of authenticity and infusing its worth into the lives of the audience. I believe ovations are not only for the person with the microphone, they're also a powerful affirmation for those offering the ovation. In this case, it was the audience's recognition of what author and storyteller Clarissa Pinkola Estes refers to as "standing up and showing your soul."

During the conference, I met many wonderful women, including a woman whose legacy intersected with mine, Konji Sebati.

From the moment I met her, she felt like a sister. For the duration of the conference, I knew her only as Konji, as she had introduced herself to me. Afterward, I learned that she was a prominent physician, well known for HIV/AIDS work in South Africa and had since become the South African ambassador to Switzerland.

In the short time that I spent in her humble and remarkable presence, Dr. Sebati invited me to speak at an event that she would host the following summer, a tribute to the women whose anti-apartheid protests struck early chords in the death knell that would eventually lead to the dismantling of apartheid. Without hesitation, I accepted Dr. Sebati's invitation to speak, intuitively recognizing a deep kinship with a cause oblivious to place or time, for injury and triumph anywhere is an injury and triumph everywhere. When I asked her, "Why me?" she said, "Because you are so passionate. When you told the stories about your life in the segregated South, they were so vivid and yet there was no trace of hatred." Then she asked only half-jokingly, "Are you sure you aren't from South Africa?" I smiled in reply, knowing instinctively that soul is no respecter of place.

WE ARE THE ONES: THEN AND NOW

On August 9, 1956, twenty thousand stouthearted South African women of all races gathered from all parts of the country to march on the Union Buildings in the capital city of Pretoria. The women staged the march to protest the atrocious pass laws, which had been in effect in South Africa for several generations. Among the many horrors of apartheid, the passes symbolized perhaps the most cruel aspect of oppression—influx control, a policy that relegated husbands into the menial role of migrant worker and made their wives into virtual widows. These unjust laws deprived children of their fathers and robbed everyone of their basic inheritance, their birthright—the right to live in a stable family unit.

The 1956 women's march was the culmination of many years of planning and organizing, including a march on the government buildings the previous year. The women marched on the Union Buildings to present to Prime Minister Johannes Gerhardus Strijdom their petitions against the pass laws, petitions that contained more than one hundred thousand signatures from citizens of South Africa and a multitude of other nations from all over the world. As part of their demonstration, the women sang freedom songs, including a song written especially for this particular occasion: "Now you have touched the women, Strijdom! You have struck a rock. You will be crushed!" (*Wathint' abafazi, Strijdom! Wathint' imbokodo uzo Kafa!*) The rock that had been struck was the rock of legacy.

The women rose up because of the horror and devastation that the pass laws had wreaked on the family. For several generations, women had been left in isolation to raise their families, to be the heads of their households. Season upon season, year after year, decade after decade, the family unit that had survived for millennia was detonated, destabilized, and ultimately destroyed in a mere half-century by these inhumane laws. The South African women had had enough. The disturbance was too great, and the future facing their children and their children's children provided the catalyst to propel the women headlong into what can only be called an audacious act of salvation, an act that would intercede on the vicious legacy bestowed by the Boer government and restore a legacy of dignity and respect.

In August 2006, against this historical backdrop, I had the privilege to present the opening address at the gathering hosted by Dr. Sebati to celebrate the fiftieth anniversary of the South African Women's March on the Union Buildings in Pretoria. I shared the dais with Dr. Sebati and other dignitaries, including Dr. Ruth Mompati, one of the co-organizers of the 1956 march. Now in her mid-eighties, except for a crown of snow-white hair she looked like a woman several decades younger.

I asked Dr. Mompati what gave her and her South African sisters the courage to conceive and the commitment to carry out such a subversive and dangerous mission. She looked at me in a way that I imagined she must have looked at the women whose hearts were galvanized by her great soul those many years ago.

Though I do not recall Dr. Mompati's precise words, I recall the spirit of them. With fire in her eyes and ferocity in her voice, she said, "Courage! Courage? We didn't need courage. We organized and sacrificed, we withstood humiliation and persecution, we went to prison and were exiled, we risked our lives and lost some of our sisters [and brothers, too,] along the way—not because we had courage. We simply did what we had to do. Why did we stand up to the white apartheid government? We did it because we were mothers!"

Dr. Mompati and her formidable phalanx of twenty thousand mothers were not theorizing about legacy as a philosophical or intellectual concept. Theirs was the brute, roiling force of legacy denied, derailed, a force as relentless and adamant as it was necessary and redemptive. In taking a stand not merely for themselves, this company of women who stood up for the sake of their children and their children's children became Woman, Mother, True Voice for those whose voices had been systematically silenced, whose voices would have remained unheard without these benefactors of goodwill, vision, hope, and triumph.

Surely, Dr. Mompati and her companions knew that God was waiting on them, that He needed their help to transform the legacy, to change the conversation, to shift the context, to sing a new song on behalf of the present generation and the generations to follow. Not only did these midwives heat the water and bring in the towels, they severed the cord that kept them bound in apartheid's stranglehold. These women were and continue to be exemplars of legacy living, assuming authority and therefore victory over tomorrow by acting with purpose and intention today.

When we celebrate the women who marched on the Union Buildings in 1956, we celebrate ordinary women who acted as any mother would who was hell-bent on saving her children. These women who acted as stewards, as guardians of the past and acolytes of the future. These women who were determined to create a new story, a new ethos for the sake of the current generation and the generations to come. These women who acted in an ordinary way in an extraordinary time.

Social activist and acclaimed scholar and poet June Jordan celebrates the power of the Sacred Promise of legacy and the soul of Woman in her rousing poetic tribute, which is simply and eloquently called "Poem for South African Women."

> Our own shadows disappear as the feet of thousands
> by the tens of thousands pound the fallow land

into new dust that
rising like a marvelous pollen will be
fertile
even as the first woman whispering
imagination to the trees around her made
for righteous fruit
from such deliberate defense of life
as no other still
will claim inferior to any other safety
in the world

The whispers too they
intimate to the inmost ear of every spirit
now aroused they
carousing in ferocious affirmation
of all peaceable and loving amplitude
sound a certainly unbounded heat
from a baptismal smoke where yes
there will be fire

And the babies cease alarm as mothers
raising arms
and heart high as the stars so far unseen
nevertheless hurl into the universe
a moving force
irreversible as light years
traveling to the open eye

And who will join this standing up
and the ones who stood without sweet company
will sing and sing
back into the mountains and
if necessary
even under the sea:

we are the ones we have been waiting for.

I have had the privilege of sharing this poem with many people around the globe. Throughout the world, people identify with South Africa's liberation struggle because it is at once unique and universal. People of all cultures respond to and are inspired by acts of courage, acts of righteous defiance, acts of fierce resolve. And as appalling as apartheid was for South Africans, their struggle was and continues to be very real as well as archetypal.

By looking through the lens of South Africa's struggle, we begin to recognize that this exterior confrontation is also mirrored within, for each of us is engaged in our personal, individual struggle for liberation, the struggle to free ourselves from the exile of our perceived limitations and constraints.

In our complex, global village, we all need reminders and encouragement, especially in the face of social injustice, that indeed "we are the ones we have been waiting for." Jordan's closing words offer an irresistible invitation to take off our robes of inadequacy, inferiority, and insufficiency, and lay them down on the altar of self-compassion so that we might forgive, surrender, and enter fully into the heart of legacy.

As allies in the perennial struggle for freedom, national or personal, we must remember the sage counsel of the elders, including these questions adapted from Elder Hillel: *If not you, who? If not now, when?*

AFFIRMATIONS: I'M DOING IT!

- I enjoy helping others.
- I am making the kind of impact I want to make.
- I keep my focus on the common good.
- I am committed to a cause beyond myself.
- I am committed to creating a positive future for others.
- I am intentional about the legacy I am creating.
- I want the next chapter of my life to count for something.

(Continued)

- I am committed to ensuring a better future for children.
- I understand that my actions will affect people I may never know.
- I know that someone or something is depending on me and my contributions.
- I am consciously and intentionally living my legacy now.

If you empower a woman, you empower a family, you empower a nation.
ANONYMOUS

PART THREE

I Am an Instrument of Soul

TAKE A CLOSER LOOK AT THE POWER of the Sacred Promises in action. See how they support you in your personal relationships, work relationships, and world work.

In Part Two, you experienced the Sacred Promises in action and began to integrate them into your life. Now that you understand how the Sacred Promises work both separately and together, you are ready to take the next step. In Part Three, you will learn how to apply your new model for living to the many facets of your life.

Part Three underscores the book's basic premise: if you want the world to be different, you must begin with yourself. In Chapters Eleven through Thirteen, we begin with the most important relationship of all, your relationship with yourself. We then gradually move outward to your relationships with friends and family, work, community, and the world.

When you wear your soul on the outside, you declare yourself as a leader, a model, a champion for soul. To nurture and care for your soul, Chapter Fourteen discusses resources for your life path of legacy living. Chapter Fifteen features stories about individuals who accepted the dare to follow their passion and calling, who have chosen to be instruments of soul. I hope their stories will inspire you to find the clarity, beauty, and transformative power of your own true voice so that you too will become an instrument of soul.

CHAPTER 11

The Sacred Promises and Right Relationships

I don't love anything more than hearing my own voice. It's a personal adoration. Listening to my recordings is like filling your pores with inspiration, and where better to get it from than yourself, because that substance is a combination of everyone who contributed something, your mama, your papa, the community, your teachers, everybody and everything.
LEONTYNE PRICE

I imagine myself living a life so rewarding that I'm living to my highest potential: I feel balanced healthy, fulfilled, and whole.

THE FUNDAMENTAL TASK IN ANY RELATIONSHIP is first to be in right relationship with yourself, which will enable you to do the same with others.

Imagine yourself—one year from now—
living the life of your highest dreams where you
are balanced, healthy, fulfilled, and whole.

The Invitation

Choose up to three Sacred Promises and describe how you
can apply what you know about them to *manifest*
what you want and claim the life you imagine in your right
relationship with yourself.
For example...

if you choose the Sacred Promise of vision, describe how your understanding of this promise can help you create your personal vision for the kind of relationships and life you want to create for yourself.

Before you continue reading this chapter, take time to reflect on *The Invitation,* and write your responses in your notebook or journal. If you complete only one or two descriptions of how you would apply the Sacred Promises to create the kind of relationship you desire, that's fine—for now. The goal is to begin to apply what you are learning. Only by applying and integrating your learning will you internalize the power of the Sacred Promises and fully comprehend how they can transform your life.

PUT YOUR OWN OXYGEN MASK ON FIRST!

If you want to learn about and develop yourself—your strengths and horizons for growth—there is no better place than in the crucible of relationship. Whether it is with a trusted friend, spouse, sibling, parent, child, mentor, work, money, or our environment, relationships help us grow and mature emotionally, intellectually, and spiritually.

To have healthy, fulfilling, sustainable relationships of any kind, the most essential relationship of all is the one you develop with yourself. Getting in right relationship with yourself or anyone else is a process and it requires only one thing, and that is love. If this sounds simple, it is—but simple isn't always easy. To have the kind of love required to be in right relationship with yourself and others, you must **value yourself**, hold a **realistic and balanced view of yourself**, and possess **humility**. When you embrace these qualities in yourself, then you can do so in your relationship with others.

As noted author Deepak Chopra recognizes, love is often mistaken for pleasure, especially in our culture. He wisely advises us not to "confuse pleasure with love. There are many things that give pleasure—playing cards, watching television—with very little love in them. Love certainly brings pleasure but in a more profound way. Carrying a meal to a shut-in is an act of love that is far more pleasurable than watching television, and there is much more to learn from such an action in terms of sharing, compassion, and understanding."

Value Yourself

At the heart of it, love is about value, or worth. To love yourself, you must value yourself and have a solid sense of your self worth. This requires that you know who you are, which includes being informed about your background and history. Exploring your cultural and family history can help you understand why you think and behave the way you do, why you invest time and energy in certain people and causes and not in others, why you care about some things and have little or no interest in others, why you celebrate certain traditions and customs, and so on.

Learning about yourself will also help you understand who and what is of worth, or value, to you. When you learn to relate in a right way with yourself, you can transfer that learning and apply it in relating to another person in a right and worthy way. When you relate in an adverse way with another person, you are also relating in an adverse way with yourself. The same holds true for any relationship, including your relations with other living things, our environment, and non-living things. In other words, how you value and treat yourself is reflected in how you value and treat everyone and everything else in your life.

Years ago, I worked with a woman who seemed mindful of her personal choices as reflected in how she dressed, how she spoke, how she presented herself to others, and so on. We occasionally traveled together for business. One afternoon in New York City after lunch, she offered me a peppermint. She proceeded to unwrap hers and promptly tossed her wrapper to the sidewalk. When I registered my surprise, she nonchalantly said, "Oh, this is New York City. Nobody takes care of their trash here." On the surface, this may seem like a small thing, but consider how this choice was a reflection of her soul.

View Yourself Realistically

The biggest challenge in learning how to relate to yourself and others occurs when you overvalue or undervalue yourself, what psychologists call self-esteem. The essence of self-esteem is to have a realistic, balanced view or assessment of yourself. An imbalanced view leads to either an inflated or deflated sense of who you are. If you view yourself too highly, you have an inflated sense of self. Conversely, if your self-assessment or opinion of yourself is unrealistically low, you have a deflated view of yourself.

How you view or assess yourself inevitably spills over into how you view others, and this will affect your relationships. If you have an imbalanced view of yourself, you will transfer that to your other relationships. When you have a healthy, balanced view of yourself, you will view others in the same way.

What manifests as a problem in your relationship with your friend, spouse, son, coworker, or the clerk at the grocery store is that you *or* the other person has an unrealistically high or low assessment of yourself or himself. Imagine how problems can quickly compound when both persons in the relationship have an imbalanced view of themselves—let alone what can happen in relationships between more than two people! The same holds true for issues that surface in families, groups, schools, community, and organizational settings, as well as between members of the opposite sex, different generations, races, ethnic groups, and nations.

Humble Yourself

As you set goals to be in right relationship with yourself, focus on humility—an aspect of love that says, "Don't try to fix or change others. Your job is to stay focused on you and your development and growth. The ground of your being, the heart of who you are is rooted in love." Humility is about kindness and caring. It's not about winning or prevailing over someone or something. Humility says, "I honor and respect you. I may disagree with you, but I also care for you and value you in the same way that I care for and value myself." Frederick Buechner puts it this way: "True humility doesn't consist of thinking ill of yourself but not thinking of yourself much differently from the way you'd be apt to think of anybody else."

As you develop and grow in right relationship with yourself, remember that it is a part of your lifelong journey toward wholeness. Also, remember to be gracious with yourself, take time to reflect on your progress, and celebrate your victories along the way—however large or small.

THE SACRED PROMISES IN ACTION

How can the Sacred Promises help you learn about yourself and flourish in your relationships? Several years ago, in search of a more balanced and fulfilled life, Rachel attended one of my workshops. A few months ago, she shared what she has learned about herself in her relationship journey of the past few years.

Born and raised in Germany, Rachel had created strong barriers against her painful memories of the time before she and her family emigrated to the United States. To keep her memories at bay, she had unconsciously created in her mind and heart what she called "The Abyss of Before and After My Emigration." For Rachel, this Abyss was a powerfully concrete and visceral image.

> It was a cataclysmically deep and black place not to be leapt across for many unspoken reasons. When you asked us to express gratitude about our past and explore our family of origin, I froze. I had blocked out so many memories of my homeland, and I did not feel close to my family of origin any longer.

During your course, the Sacred Promise of legacy grabbed my attention. Until that moment I never thought that anything I did or thought would be worthwhile to pass on. I had this feeling that the things I liked to do—painting, making collages, writing stories and poems, creating hand-made books, and keeping a journal—were just ways of indulging myself.

As Rachel began to value what she calls her "playful arts" and share them, she was delighted when she found that they also gave solace to others. In the several years since completing the workshop, Rachel has edited and compiled her poems and will soon have her first poetry book published.

The more I thought about the kind of legacy I wanted to leave for my children and grandchildren, the more I realized that my European past is a very important part of it. As I explored the Sacred Promises, something inside me shifted and I began to see this time in my life in a very different way.

When I remembered The Abyss, it shocked me and woke me up. . . . As I wrote in my journal, wrote poems, and created collages about it, I became more familiar with this forbidden place. I was able to see and feel and then shape the sometimes very painful thoughts and memories into something beautiful and healing.

As the weeks passed by, I began to realize just how important legacy is. I also had a growing awareness of what kind of a legacy I was leaving by living without examining things. The thing that shook me a bit was the clay figure, the sculpture you invited us to create to help us better understand and deal with our inner critic. I created the sculpture with little odds and ends and trinkets. To my surprise, it was not lying down on its construction paper background. It was standing up and obviously talking, almost as if from a pulpit.

I realized I had things to get on with and things that needed to be said. And you can't do that lying down. So I began saying them to myself. I began saying them to my sister in Germany as well, sending her some of my poems, even though they are written in English and she has to look up words in the dictionary. . . .

It was the desire to leave a legacy of love and healing that opened the doors of communication between my sister and me. She may have had her door wide open all the while, but I did not realize it. I could not get through the door due to my own need to keep that part and the pain of that part of my life locked away.

I realized that I cannot be true to myself and to the legacy I want to leave for my children and children's children if I don't embrace all of my life, past and present.

These days, Rachel is working on a second book of poems about growing up in Germany after the war. She and her sister call one another weekly and exchange e-mails in between. "There is no more vibration of holding back between us," says Rachel. In fact, she is considering the possibility of purchasing the piece of property directly across from her sister's small home, "so that I can spend longer periods of time near her. We are imagining ourselves running back and forth between our gardens, from front door to front door, creating a legacy of laughter and love."

Rachel is profoundly grateful for her newfound sense of self worth, which has transformed how she views herself and has nourished her daffodils-in-bloom relationship with her sister.

Two of the happiest side effects of working on my legacy were a newfound respect for myself, and also a delicious intimacy with my sister with whom I had had a strained relationship ever since I left home. A very definite part of this new ability to be intimate with my sister is that I am now able to be intimate with myself in regard to the German parts of myself that I had left behind.

LESSONS LEARNED

Understanding that the most important relationship is the one you have with yourself, Rachel transformed her vision for her life. She began with the goal of leaving a positive legacy for her children and grandchildren and recognized that to do so she would first have to change her vision of herself. By altering her vision of herself, she was able to transform her relationship with her sister. Notice that Rachel did not try to fix or change her sister. By focusing on being in right relationship with herself, she is now a testament that "everything changes when you do."

To prepare for the next *Exercise*, reread Rachel's experience and as you do, pay attention to her recognition and application of the Sacred Promises. Then we will go on to discuss the connection between the promises and Rachel's experiences.

EXERCISE

Set aside time when you won't have any distractions, and remember to use your notebook or journal for your notes.

- Rachel says that her primary focus is the Sacred Promise of legacy. As you reread Rachel's story, notice the other promises at work in her life. Jot them down in your notebook or journal, and find two or three specific examples of the promises at work in Rachel's life.

In Rachel's experience, all the Sacred Promises and aspects of right relationship come into play. Some of the promises, such as **legacy** and **love**, stand out more than others because they are evident in what Rachel says. Review the summary in the table to see how these two promises show up in Rachel's own words. And though I have listed in a linear sequence the evidence of the promises at work, this is not the exact order in which Rachel's experience unfolded. Like anyone else's experience would be, hers was anything but sequential and linear! Rachel's experience revealed itself in the same way that life unfolds—in circles and spirals and loops.

Sacred Promise	In Rachel's Own Words
Legacy	*During your course, the Sacred Promise of legacy grabbed my attention. The more I thought about the kind of legacy I wanted to leave for my children and grandchildren . . . I began to realize just how important legacy is.*
Love	*It was the desire to leave a legacy of love and healing that opened the doors of communication between my sister and me. Two of the happiest side effects . . . were a newfound respect for myself, and also a delicious intimacy with my sister.*

Other Sacred Promises, such as **gratitude** and **integrity**, are also woven into Rachel's experience. Let's take a closer look at where and how these promises show up for Rachel and what role they play in the creative actions she takes to move herself in the direction of what she desires. As you review the summary of the Sacred Promises at work, also notice the resulting shifts as Rachel comes into right relationship with herself.

In Rachel's own words and experience, she initially encounters the Sacred Promise of **gratitude** as a kind of confrontation: "When you asked us to express gratitude about our past . . . I froze." Though Rachel cannot express her gratitude for her past just yet, her recognition of this is crucial. In this moment of truth, she takes a step of faith to begin a process to creatively and critically examine the "kind of legacy she was leaving by living without examining things." (Notice that the Sacred Promises of faith, creative action, and legacy are also at work here.)

Our past often holds important clues that, once explored, can help us make choices that move us toward what we want to create without hanging onto unnecessary clutter and baggage. Rachel explored many aspects of her European heritage, including her family of origin and cultural history. Both of these aspects of **gratitude** helped her acknowledge the past, better understand the present, and influence her choices about the future. (Notice that the Sacred Promises of vision and creative action are also at work here.)

Through her clay sculpture, Rachel rediscovers her own powerful voice. Instead of lying down, the sculpture stands up and gives voice to matters of the heart and soul, serving as a powerful catalyst in Rachel's quest to embrace and express her own true voice. (Notice that the Sacred Promise of integrity is also at work here.)

For Rachel, her family and cultural histories are vital links, connecting her past, present, and future. She began to appreciate previously hidden aspects of herself, which shifted her view of herself, resulting in higher self-esteem—which contributed to Rachel coming into right relationship with herself.

By connecting the familial and cultural parts of her identity, Rachel experienced the Sacred Promise of **integrity** at work. The power of this promise enabled Rachel to consciously recognize and confront her painful memories and, ultimately, to construct a bridge of healing and restoration by which she could cross the chasm—the foreboding "Abyss"—in her journey toward wholeness. "Until that moment, I never thought that anything I did or thought would be worthwhile to pass on."

Rachel had consistently dismissed her considerable gifts in what she calls the "playful arts." And by refusing to embrace these aspects of herself, she denies exquisite dimensions of her signature presence. While others recognize and acknowledge the beauty of Rachel's poems, books, and collages, she diminishes their worth, minimizing and undervaluing herself in the process. To get into right relationship with herself, she must lean in to the devotional hearth of gratitude and of love. (Notice that the Sacred Promises of love, as it relates to self-love, and creative action are also at work here.)

By examining her German roots within the context of her European heritage, Rachel can now appreciate and become intimate with the German parts of herself. These choices together with many others enable her to make significant strides toward wholeness, an aspect of **integrity** that will ultimately lead to healing Rachel's relationship with herself, her sister, and her heritage. (Notice that the Sacred Promise of creative action is at work throughout Rachel's experience as she moves toward manifesting the Sacred Promise of legacy.)

My summary of how the promises show up and are at work in Rachel's experience is just the beginning. As I mentioned earlier, all the promises are in motion for Rachel. A good next step is to review Rachel's story and those of others in earlier chapters to get a fuller sense of the promises at work and their power in shifting the persons involved. Now that the table is prepared, as you complete the next set of *Exercises*, imagine yourself at your own table.

EXERCISES

Set aside time when you won't have any distractions, and remember to use your notebook or journal for your notes.

- Put on some soothing, relaxing music. Review your notes of the Sacred Promises in Rachel's experience.
- Reflect back on the life you imagined at the beginning of this chapter, where you are in right relationship with yourself and living to your highest potential. Using Rachel's experience as a catalyst, describe how the Sacred Promises can help you in *your* journey. For example, you might write something like this:

You know, Rachel's experience helped me realize that I'd like to leave a positive legacy, too (legacy). Unlike Rachel, I have a pretty strong relationship with my family (love). Maybe too strong! If I'm not working or talking on the phone with one of my sisters, I'm driving my daughter to soccer practice, piano lessons, or a friend's house. My routine doesn't leave much time for me. I was so excited when I began to think about my life and what I wanted for myself (vision).

- Write for at least twenty minutes—without stopping if you can. Do not stop to read what you're writing. Just let it flow.

Congratulations! You have made a number of significant choices—creative actions all—in imagining and claiming the future you desire. Now that you have completed *The Invitation* at the beginning of this chapter and the *Exercises*, take time to celebrate yourself and your accomplishment. You deserve it. Take a walk. Listen to your favorite music. Watch a movie. Visit a museum.

In earlier chapters, you were introduced to *Affirmations* to validate your exploration of the Sacred Promises. As you take the next steps to manifest the life you imagine, you will continue to benefit from the affirmations that say, "I'm Doing It!" However, manifesting the future you desire requires you to make a covenant—a sacred commitment—with yourself. The *Promises to Keep* that follow will help you as you dare to wear your soul on the outside and pass your blessings on to others.

PROMISES TO KEEP

I, _____, am committed to changing the only person I can change—myself. I am also committed to manifesting a joyous life where I am healthy, balanced, fulfilled, and whole.
To do so, I will:

- Hold my personal vision in which I imagine a rewarding life for myself.
- Take positive, life-affirming actions toward the life I imagine, so that I will manifest it.

- Commit to nurturing and developing the most important relationship of all, which is with myself. This means that I will value myself, view myself realistically, and be humble.
- Act as a steward on behalf of the future, and pass it on.

- _____

- _____

- _____

Faithfully yours,

_____

_____

Life takes on shape and meaning when a person is able to transcend the barriers of personal survival and become a unique conduit for its vital energy.
ROSAMUND STONE ZANDER AND BENJAMIN ZANDER

CHAPTER 12

The Sacred Promises at Work

Humility says there were people before me who found the path. I'm a road builder. For those who are yet to come, I seem to be finding the path and they will be road builders. That keeps one humble. Love keeps one humble.
MAYA ANGELOU

I imagine myself working in a setting where every day is extraordinary, my contribution is deeply connected to my life's larger purposes, and I am making a positive difference in others' lives.

THE GOALS OF LIFE AND WORK ARE THE SAME: to fall in love with who you are and ensure that your work serves your life. This means that your work is in harmony with who you are and what you most care about.

Imagine yourself working in a setting where
you are not only passionately engaged but you
are also free to be your authentic, brilliant, joyous self.

The Invitation

Choose up to three Sacred Promises and describe how you can apply
what you know about them to create the kind of work life you want so
that you can be authentic, fully engaged, bring forth the brilliance of
your *signature presence,* and have a blast doing it.
For example…

if you choose the Sacred Promise of integrity, describe how your
understanding of this promise can help you create or discover the
kind of work and work setting that meets your needs. This would
be work where you can't wait to get out of bed in the morning,
and you're working with people where you can be your true self.
When you lose all track of time while working, this typically means
your work and needs line up.

Before you continue reading this chapter, take time to reflect
on *The Invitation,* and write your responses in your notebook or
journal. If you complete only one or two descriptions of how
you would apply the Sacred Promises to create the kind of work
life you desire, that's fine—for now. The goal is to begin to apply
what you are learning. Only by applying and integrating your
learning will you internalize the power of the Sacred Promises
and fully comprehend how they can transform your life.

MAKE THE INVISIBLE VISIBLE

Most of us spend a good portion of our waking hours working.
We pour our precious intellectual, emotional, and spiritual energy
into work at least five days a week, eight hours a day, not counting "after hours" time connecting to our work via computers, cell
phones, and other electronic devices. Well over three-quarters of
us work in jobs where the only satisfaction is our paycheck. No
love, let alone passion. No happiness, not to mention joy.

It doesn't have to be this way. You can experience passion and joy—at work! When you dare to wear your soul on the outside, you are clear about and honor your values, you are the same person at work as elsewhere, you make your work serve your life, and you reach out and encourage others along the way. You can find your center, core values, and true voice by exploring what deeply matters to you, and then discover how what you love to do connects with what the world needs to have done. Ask yourself: Does my work feed my soul's hunger? Or does it merely feed my ego?

VALUE YOUR VALUES

Values are the bedrock of our lives; they undergird and shape our character, attitudes, beliefs, and choices. Values simultaneously say "This is what and who matters to me" and "This is how I want to be known." When you speak and act from your values, you will be in right relationship with yourself, and others will see you as authentic, reliable, and trustworthy. They will know that they can count on you to step up and be courageous when faced with the inevitable challenges of daily work life.

Unexamined, our values will obscure us from ourselves. When you don't take the time to identify and understand what you care about, what matters to you, you wall off important parts of yourself. When revealed, your values act as a compass for you, providing direction to keep you focused on where you're headed in your work and life. Cassidy, a talented young entrepreneur in one of my courses on creativity and right livelihood, is fond of saying, "A vision without an action plan is like an eagle without wings." Similarly, a vision without values is like a house without a foundation, a body without a soul.

TRANSFORM THE ORDINARY INTO THE EXTRAORDINARY: BEGIN WITH YOURSELF

The key to changing your work life from ordinary to extraordinary is not about what you do for work. If you are like most people, you will ask: "Is this job a good fit for me?" This is the wrong question.

A better question is: "Am I a good fit for this job?" In other words, can you drop the facade and be your true self at work? Can you show up as your authentic, brilliant, and magnificent self at work and elsewhere, or do you leave part of yourself in the parking lot, or at home?

When you value yourself and honor your values, you have the power to turn your ordinary work experience into the extraordinary every single day. Even if your work is intellectually, emotionally, or physically exacting, it doesn't have to be laborious or leave you feeling exhausted. You will know that your life and work are aligned when your work renews and rewards you with emotional, intellectual, and spiritual income. If you work for a wage, your rewards will be monetary as well. You will also know that your work and life are in harmony because as you expend energy, you are reenergized. You feel joyous, and your joy benefits others, transforming the atmosphere around you. Jazz musicians would say that you are definitely in your groove, because you are vibrant, flowing, and in accord with yourself and the world. Others want to be around you. Some simply want to be near you to bask in your glow while others want to know what moves you so that they can experience that same stream of synchronous energy and joy.

MAKE YOUR WORK SERVE YOUR LIFE

As you become clear about your values, you may find yourself questioning your work. Does my work align with my values? Am I passionately engaged in my work? Is my work serving my life, or is my life serving my work? I recently spoke with Joyce, a coaching client who leads a large human services agency that places vulnerable children and youth with loving families. She provided a wonderful example of making her work serve her life.

> In my early years as a social worker, I realized how much I love working with children. I also recognized the critical need for skilled people to work with them. Children need adults who can advocate for them and navigate the bureaucracy of the human services system. Well, I sought out an agency that shared my values: integrity in my work and helping children become the best they can be. Children are our future!

I've been a social worker for over thirty-two years, working my way up to CEO. When people ask me when I'm going to retire, I tell them, "Never!" Of course, I will—someday. My work is so exciting. I just love what I do. What could be more rewarding than ensuring that children have a chance to become all that they can be? Sure, my work has its share of challenges. And at times I tire of the politics, but I'm always energized by working with children and families. I'd be a champion for them whether they paid me or not!

I asked Joyce what advice she would offer others, especially those just starting their careers. Without hesitation she said, "Make your life count. And realize that it's not about you. When you focus on making a difference for others, your life takes on new meaning. Also, remember to reach out to and nurture others. I've been very fortunate to work with supervisors and peers who mentored and encouraged me. A little support goes a long way."

Many of us crave work that aligns with who we are, but unlike Joyce, we work in jobs that are draining or, worse, deadening. Remember this: your work doesn't define who you are; *you* do. If you have little or no choice about where you work, you are still in charge of you—your emotional, physical, intellectual, and spiritual self. If you can't change your job, change your focus and your attitude. By doing so, you will transform your circumstances from mundane to meaningful, perhaps even marvelous.

Begin by applying the Sacred Promises. Choose to be grateful, faithful, and loving. Start small and keep it simple. Think of as many reasons as you can to express gratitude for your work. You can begin by being grateful that you have a job, even if it's one you complain about! Find a reason to compliment your boss or a coworker. Bring them fresh flowers, just because. If you're short on cash, smiles are free. Smile at everyone you see today—you never know who is having a rough day and needs the harbor of your smile.

Integrate creative action outside your work as well. With every action you take, you wear your soul on the outside and shine a little light on someone else. Choose to serve others; serving others will shift your focus and strengthen your resolve to make a difference in someone else's life. Look for opportunities to be of service in your community. Serve meals at a homeless shelter, work at your local food bank, or join a team of volunteers to clean up a local park. Help an elderly person load groceries into the car. Set a timer for fifteen minutes every other day, and clean your bookshelves or closets, giving away gently used books, shoes, or clothes to an organization that will pass them on. Write thank-you notes to your parents, children, or friends. If you are inclined to wait until you have reached a certain level, position, or financial freedom, don't. Now is always the right time to reach out to others, to pass your blessings on, to make a difference in someone else's life.

Your choices reflect your values and signature presence, at work and beyond. Remember that your significance isn't determined by your job or career. Your significance is determined by you, by who you are and what you value, regardless of your circumstances. You may not receive the kind of satisfaction from work that Joyce does, but with clarity about your values, knowing that you are in charge of yourself, and taking the Sacred Promises to heart, you will achieve the kind of deep satisfaction that only comes from within.

THE SACRED PROMISES IN ACTION

Maggie is the executive director of a foundation for one of the largest health services networks in the United States. Though her work is demanding, and she has a full personal schedule as the single parent of two teenage daughters, Maggie is thrilled to be working in the job of her dreams. When others ask her about her good fortune, she assures them that what might look on the surface like "overnight success" is not. Maggie says, "It's been a long road to get to this place," a journey that began back in her childhood.

> When I was a little girl, my mother was director of nursing in a long-term care facility right across the street from our family home. I spent many years volunteering and just hanging out there. I learned to play the piano and how to do embroidery there. Sometimes I'd go shopping for the residents. It was like my second family. Several guys who worked in the facility's wood shop even built me a doll house.

While many in Maggie's family thought she should follow in her mother's footsteps and become a nurse, she was drawn to communications, where she felt she could influence a broader spectrum of people than she could working with people one on one.

Before finding an open door in health care, Maggie worked for almost twenty years in advertising and in marketing and communications for the health insurance industry. As she moved up the ranks and assumed greater responsibility and oversaw larger budgets, Maggie became increasingly uncomfortable about the millions of dollars being spent on externally focused competitive activities, while so many people went without access to basic health care services.

> I started having a lot of internal conflict about this, so much so that I wasn't feeling right about doing my job. Meanwhile, I was going through a difficult marriage. I decided to strengthen my faith and turned to my faith community as a way to cope and find my way.
>
> For many years, I prayed about these personal and work conflicts and got better and better at listening to what I was being called to pay attention to. I stayed "in" the conflict and really held true to my belief that something different was meant for me. I went to lots of public forums and workshops to gain exposure to personal improvement ideas that other people were finding to be meaningful and important. On the personal front, I joined a couple of support-prayer groups.
>
> I had to quiet myself big time. I learned to do this through centering prayer, journaling, and early morning reading before the kids would get up. . . . Once I was able to be calm and not also be reactive when in conflicted situations, I was able to listen, be guided, and take meaningful steps with the faith that—as in dance—when you take a leap that the floor will actually rise up to meet you!
>
> The power behind all this was love. Over time, as I went to church more and more, I began not to feel so entirely alone and self-sufficient. "I can do this" used to be my motto. Now it's "Love will make a way." The power of the love in my support-prayer group and in services when we held hands and sang the "Our Father" was almost too great, and yet I began to feel that I belonged and that this love was actually for me, too. In addition, I truly came to understand the love of God and that in faith all things are possible.

Then one day, I saw the advertisement for my current position, foundation executive director and director of public relations for a health care organization I had heard about for years, and I thought, "But of course."

Maggie admitted that the first few weeks were not an easy transition. "I didn't foresee how big a leap it would be from my prior world into this one." In addition, she had to handle several pressing staff issues—individuals who were either not accepting of her or not working up to par. On the personal front, Maggie was going through a divorce and raising her two teens full time on her own. "I felt overwhelmed and truly couldn't imagine handling any additional conflict at work."

Deciding that she was not the right person for her position at that particular time, Maggie resigned that position to take another job, returning to the health insurance industry. She was gone for all of one day.

When I got to this other organization, I took one look around and wondered, where are all the residents—the individuals we were truly benefiting?

I quickly realized that the power of the mission of the organization I had left behind was far greater than the difficulties I had been facing, and I called my boss and expressed that I had made a mistake and that I would need her support in making changes if I came back.

She hadn't turned in my departure paperwork, and I returned the next day. I'm so glad I did. Here in this community, I felt nurtured enough to pull through both the work and the personal challenges that I was going through.

Maggie admits that her work is difficult at times, but the personal rewards are extraordinary. Not only is she doing what she is passionate about, she gets to work within the community of residents for whom her organization provides services. She says, "And the bonus is that I feel so integrated as a person and within this amazing community." Grateful for her faith life that has carried her through difficult circumstances, and for values that are in synch with her work, Maggie is also delighted that her choices have set the stage for the next chapter in her life.

I have met a man who seems to know and love me because of who I am and how that is expressed in my integration of my faith, work, community, and person.

I hadn't been looking, but I had prayed that I might again share my life with someone. And, I've been true to myself over these last six years without the worry of needing to define, control, or direct the future.

My life is better than I would have ever imagined.

LESSONS LEARNED

Maggie recognized that she was caught up in a dilemma common to many of us. As a director of marketing and strategic planning in the health insurance industry, she was working in a role that was not attuned with her personal vision or values. The conflict in her internal values at work was mirrored in the dynamics of her personal relationship as she confronted the challenges in her marriage.

As she sought an anchor to support her through the storms of her professional and personal life, Maggie recognized that her reactivity might actually be an ally and teacher. Rather than avoiding or running away from her conflict, she leaned in to it and held fast to her belief that something new and different awaited her.

To prepare for the next *Exercise*, reread Maggie's experience, and as you do, pay attention to her recognition and application of the Sacred Promises. Then we will go on to discuss the connection between the promises and Maggie's experiences.

EXERCISE

Set aside time when you won't have any distractions, and remember to use your notebook or journal for your notes.

- Maggie's initial focus was to strengthen her faith and turn to her faith community as she found her way. These creative actions align with the Sacred Promises of faith and integrity. Notice the other promises at work in Maggie's life. Jot them down in your notebook or journal, including two or three specific examples of the promises in action in Maggie's experience.

In Maggie's experience, all of the Sacred Promises and aspects of values, authenticity, making your work serve your life, and encouraging others come into play. Some of the promises, such as **faith** and **integrity**, will stand out more than others. Review the summary in the table to see how these two promises show up and are evident in what Maggie says. And remember that the sequential list is to illustrate and glean the lessons in the promises. The exact order of Maggie's multilayered experience was anything but sequential and linear! Maggie's experience revealed itself in the same way that life unfolds—in circles and spirals and loops.

Sacred Promise	In Maggie's Own Words
Faith	*Meanwhile, I was going through a difficult marriage. I decided to strengthen my faith and turned to my faith community. . . . Once I was able to be calm and not also be reactive . . . I was able to listen, be guided, and take meaningful steps with the faith that—as in dance—when you take a leap that the floor will actually rise up to meet you!*
Integrity	*I started having a lot of internal conflict about this, so much so that I wasn't feeling right about doing my job. Then one day, I saw an advertisement for my current position . . . for a health care organization I had heard about for years, and I thought, "But of course."*

Other Sacred Promises, such as **vision** and **creative action**, are also woven into Maggie's experience. Let's take a closer look at where and how these promises show up for Maggie and what role they play in moving her toward personal and professional fulfillment and wholeness.

Maggie's experience of the Sacred Promise of **vision** is evident early on. In her struggle to cope and find her way, she takes the **creative action** of clearing the fog by strengthening her faith and finding a community of belonging. As Maggie recognized, it is difficult to create a new **vision** for yourself when your current view is obscured by fog—in her case, the fog of conflict at work and in her marriage: "For many years, I prayed about these personal and work conflicts and got better and better at listening to what I was being called to pay attention to." (Notice that the Sacred Promise of faith is also at work here.)

Shortly after arriving at her new organization, Maggie quickly recognized the disconnect between her personal **vision** and values and the apparent **vision** and values of her new organization. "I took one look around and wondered, where are all the residents—the individuals we're truly benefiting?"

Maggie made the shift from her current reality to a new **vision** of possibility for herself. Her take-charge attitude and other **creative actions** make an authoritative list for care and restoration of the heart and soul:

- Searching for and finding a faith community
- Listening and responding to the call of her powerful inner voice
- Simultaneously staying in the conflict and remaining true to her **vision**
- Joining support-prayer groups
- Being in a loving, supportive work community
- Exploring meaningful relationships and new ideas in her profession
- Valuing herself through solitude and journaling, reading, praying, and singing
- Taking time to quiet herself and manage her reactivity
- Humbly acknowledging to her boss her mistake in resigning her position
- Asking for appropriate support to face her work challenges

The significance of even one of these **creative actions** is immense. When layered and appropriately sequenced, their combined effect is synergistic, which means that 1 plus 2 no longer equals 3; it equals 5, 9, or 16. The net result is that Maggie opened the door to a better life than she had ever imagined. (Notice that the Sacred Promises of faith, **vision**, and love are also at work here.)

My summary of how the promises show up and are at work in Maggie's experience is just the beginning. A good next step is to review Maggie's experience and that of others in earlier chapters to get a fuller sense of the promises at work and their power in shifting the people involved. Now that the table is prepared, as you complete the next set of *Exercises*, imagine yourself at your own table.

EXERCISES

Set aside time when you won't have any distractions, and remember to use your notebook or journal for your notes.

- Put on your favorite music. Light a candle with the specific intention of sending a little of your own light into the world. Review your notes on the Sacred Promises in Maggie's experience.
- Reflect back on the life you imagined at the beginning of this chapter, where you are working in a setting where you are free to be your authentic self. Using Maggie's experience as a catalyst, describe how the Sacred Promises can help you in *your* journey to transform your work life from ordinary to extraordinary.

Congratulations! You have made a number of significant choices—creative actions all—in imagining and claiming the future you desire. Now that you have completed *The Invitation* at the beginning of this chapter and the *Exercises*, take time to celebrate yourself and your accomplishment. You deserve it. Buy yourself some fresh flowers. Visit the zoo. Go to a play. Invite a friend.

In earlier chapters, you were introduced to *Affirmations* to validate your exploration of the Sacred Promises. As you take the next steps to manifest the life you imagine, you will continue to benefit from the affirmations that say, "I'm Doing It!" However, manifesting the future you desire requires you to make a covenant—a sacred commitment—with yourself. The *Promises to Keep* that follow will help you as you dare to wear your soul on the outside and pass your blessings on to others.

PROMISES TO KEEP

I, _____, am committed to falling in love with myself and my work. I will also ensure that my work and the setting I work in are in harmony with my values.
To do so, I will:

- Hold my personal vision for my work life where every day is extraordinary because I can be authentic and fully engaged.

- Take positive, life-affirming actions each day to ensure that my values and my work life are aligned.
- Commit to nurturing and developing myself, with the goal of making my work serve my life. This means that I will be authentic in my relationships with others and seek work settings that fit my values, as I boldly and humbly wear my soul on the outside.
- Act as a steward on behalf of the future, and pass it on.

- _____

- _____

- _____

Faithfully yours,

_____

I didn't want to write about somebody who turned out to be a star 'cause most people don't turn out to be stars. And yet their lives are just as sweet and just as rich as any others and often they are richer and sweeter.
GWENDOLYN BROOKS

CHAPTER 13

The Sacred Promises and World Work

> *Every man must decide whether he will walk in
> the light of creative altruism or the darkness of
> destructive selfishness. Life's most persistent and
> urgent question is, what are you doing for others?*
> MARTIN LUTHER KING JR.

I imagine living a vibrant life where I'm in right
relationship with myself, aligned with my values, and
making a meaningful contribution to the world.

THE PRIMARY GOAL AND CHALLENGE OF WORLD WORK is to be of
service to others, and to do so in a way that simultaneously honors
and blurs the differences that threaten to keep us separated from
ourselves and one another.

Imagine yourself making a defining contribution
to your world, co-creating a phenomenal future
for generations to come.

The Invitation

Choose up to three Sacred Promises and describe how you can apply
what you know about them to manifest your hopes and dreams as a
steward of the future.
For example…

if you choose the Sacred Promise of faith, describe how your understanding of this promise can be a resource to you as you support others—family members and other loved ones, neighbors, coworkers, civic leaders, and even complete strangers. Ask yourself, "Am I offering myself with a heart of service?"

Before you continue reading this chapter, take time to reflect on *The Invitation,* and write your responses in your notebook or journal. If you complete only one or two descriptions of how you would apply the Sacred Promises to create the kind of community, the kind of world you desire, that's fine—for now. The goal is to begin to apply what you are learning. Only by applying and integrating your learning will you internalize the power of the Sacred Promises and fully comprehend how they can transform your life.

THROW A BETTER PARTY

As we collectively reimagine the world, we increase our awareness of just how deeply our lives are intertwined. Even as we weave a wondrous web of interconnection, wholeness, and possibility, we leave behind an astonishing trail of cynicism and unnecessary borders, a mosaic of brokenness and betrayal. In the face of such daunting challenges, perhaps you wonder, "What can one individual do to make any difference in the world, let alone make a defining contribution?"

Take heart. You're already doing "it." If you've gotten this far in this book, you're already making a defining difference, because you're taking creative action in your own life to be of service to others.

World work is about legacy with an attitude of service—about being of use to someone else or in service to a cause beyond yourself with no strings attached, or, as my colleague Peter Block says, "with no expectation of reward." World work says, "If you want to leave the world a little bit better off than the way you found it, then it's up to you to do so." And it's up to each one of us to use our innate creativity along with our other gifts, talents, and skills to create the kind of world we want; a world of devotion to one another, not divisions; a world of astonishing possibility for all, not merely the privileged few. As my friend Rick Ingrasci says, "If you want to create a new culture, throw a better party." Your party can be simple and close to home, in service to family and friends; it can also extend beyond. Both will be life-changing.

World work starts when you make a positive change in your own life. As you learned in Chapters Eleven and Twelve, you begin by first being in right relationship with yourself and aligned with your values. Arrayed in your garment of creative action and your attitude of service, you make yourself useful to others.

Whether your acts of service are for your loved ones or complete strangers, everything you do affects the world in some way; you will make an impact. Don't be seduced into believing that the farther you cast your net in service to others, the better. How many you affect and how far away they are is beside the point. World work is not about numbers or distance; it says, "You do what you can, with what you have, wherever you are." World work doesn't keep a scorecard. What matters is that you offer your skills, talents, and gifts to be of use in service to someone or something beyond yourself.

World work is about love. Service is an act of love. To love and to serve is to align yourself with the ethos of Marge Piercy's lovely poem "To Be of Use," in which she reminds us that just as "the pitcher cries for water to carry," the human heart cries "for work that is real." And, I would add, it cries for work that is infused with caring that is other-centered, not self-centered.

WORLD WORK
CAN HAPPEN ANYWHERE

World work is a way to recognize and use your incredible power to be of service to others, thereby transforming yourself and the world around you. It can take place anywhere and with anyone.

You can make a difference right in your own family, neighborhood, community, or city. Miguel, an accountant, shops for groceries once a week. Each time he shops, he buys a few extra loaves of bread and canned goods and puts them in the bin for a local food bank. Diane, a high school math teacher, volunteers as a tutor three days a week after school. She says that she really enjoys being with the students: "Sometimes after we're done with math, I just hang out with them and talk teen talk."

Photographer and writer Joanne Petrina devoted several years to painstakingly document the deeply personal and moving testimonies of individuals in a Seattle area neighborhood that is home to one of the largest immigrant and refugee communities in the United States. As the heart of this community is altered by the construction of a massive public transit system, Joanne spoke with and captured the stories of her neighbors—all first-generation immigrants—not only to honor their heritage and culture, but also to raise awareness about their concerns and challenges, and their hopes and dreams.

Joanne met with and photographed a number of adults and youth, including Sahra Farah, formerly of Somalia and now a resident and community leader in this neighborhood. Sahra told Joanne about her life-changing conversation with another Somalian woman who also lived in the heart of this urban United States neighborhood.

> I decided to start my own business, so I took some college courses. On the day of the final exams, I walked out of the building and found an elderly Somalian lady who had seen me enter. She was waiting for me. I went to her, and she began to cry. She told me that she was lost, unable to find her house. I spoke with her and did not leave her until we found her house. She invited me in. She was here in the United States, but she often wondered "What am I doing here? I don't understand the culture, and I don't speak the language." She was isolated and lonely and only wanted to return to Somalia. Something happened to me that day. I realized the best thing for me to do was to help my people. I chose to work with the Somalian community. This lady changed my mind.

My neighbor Stacy got an idea from a friend to collect coats and send them to kids who have none in the mountains of Morocco. Stacy researched her idea and learned that aid sent into the country was frequently stolen before it ever reached those who most needed it. But she didn't let that stop her. Late last summer, she began to collect coats, boxes and boxes of them. In early November, she appealed to a few of her friends to help with shipping costs. Later that month, the coats were on their way to Morocco. Stacy shipped the boxes via Lufthansa Airlines. Her niece, who works for Lufthansa, intercepted them so she could take them to the kids in the mountains.

But the coats were not just a blessing for the intended kids.

A local guide helped my niece sort the coats for the kids. He spoke only a little English, and he was very poor. For his help and kindness, my niece offered him coats for his family. He couldn't believe her. He kept asking if she was sure, and she finally reassured him that she was. He took two coats only—for his children—and he cried with gratitude. Later he brought his wife who tried to thank my niece. The wife didn't speak English, but she, too, cried and cried in thanksgiving.

WORLD WORK IS THE SOUL OF SERVICE

At its best, world work occurs within the context of holding a vision for the highest good for all—for individuals in your immediate circle or network, as well as for the whole, the world. This includes you, your family, work group, organization, neighborhood, city, country, and our environment. One of my clients calls world work her service to our world family.

In our global, interconnected community, there's always something you can do, however small or large, for someone or some cause. Don't give in to feeling overwhelmed. Like Miguel and Diane, you can start small, simply, and close to home.

Reverend Johanna Wise reminds us that in the routine of our daily lives we encounter individuals from all walks of life, "who are different from ourselves: people in robes, homeless people, drug addicts, the poor, the sick, prison inmates, people with different beliefs." We must consider these people as individuals and not as a group, not as "them." When we see these individuals "as fellow human beings on life's path . . . then we will ask ourselves how can we be of service."

Reverend Wise counsels that we must not judge; we must only ask, "How can I help? How can I be of use? How can I make things better for my sister or brother?" Ultimately, world work is an act of the soul. Given the extremely powerful forces that conspire to disillusion you, if you want to resist them, world work offers a compelling alternative. For twenty-first-century citizens of a global community, Dr. Martin Luther King Jr.'s question "What are you doing for others?" is not only an urgent one to answer but also a productive and empowering one.

As you dare to express yourself in world work, remember that it begins with you. Also remember that if you live with passionate intention and are conscious about legacy, your world work is already in motion. If you are reaching out to family members, friends, coworkers, or neighbors in the spirit of service, you are making a difference. You are doing world work.

THE SACRED PROMISES IN ACTION

It seems impossible that the engaging, articulate woman who is now the executive director of Crown Academy could have been living out of her car with her two young sons, and then in a homeless shelter for several years after that. Now a respected leader in her community, Maxine Davis started Crown Academy eighteen years ago. The school is designed to meet the unique needs of children who are homeless.

Before her own firsthand experience of being homeless, Maxine was happily married to Derrick, the man of her dreams. Blessed with twin boys a couple of years after they married, she and Derrick both had solid, stable jobs and saw a bright future ahead. Maxine says, "I guess you could say we were living a good life." They bought the latest model cars, the latest, coolest computers and other electronic gadgets for themselves and their kids, and provided them with everything they thought they needed. They set aside a small amount for a "rainy day," but never really thought about saving or investing for the long-term.

During the next few years, Maxine and her family continued living their dream life. Then unexpectedly, suddenly, her life turned upside down. Maxine's dream life became a nightmare. One evening right before supper, the phone rang. Assuming it was

Derrick calling to let her know he'd been working late and would soon be home, she was surprised to hear an unfamiliar voice. Her surprise gave way to stunned silence: "All I remember him saying is '. . . State Patrol . . . Derrick . . . ambulance . . . Grand Valley Medical . . .'" Maxine later learned that her husband's car had been struck head-on by a drunk driver. Derrick had been rushed to the hospital, but his injuries were massive. The last time Maxine saw Derrick, he was in a coma. A few days later he passed away without ever regaining consciousness.

> I was devastated when my husband slipped away from me, his sons, and this world. During the months after his death, I tried to hold myself together for my boys. But I was an emotional wreck. Each night after I put the boys to bed, I put on my robe, laid down, and just cried. I hardly returned phone calls, I didn't balance my checkbook, I didn't even look at my mail . . . none of it mattered. At that time, all that mattered were my boys and my memories of my beloved soul mate.

What little family she had, Maxine couldn't find or didn't want to contact. Through no fault of her own, when she was nine years old she wound up in foster care, drifting from one group home to another until she turned eighteen and could finally be on her own. Maxine says that her stubbornness and pride kept her from accepting help from her small circle of friends. She now admits that she didn't want them to think she couldn't make it on her own.

> I ended up losing my job and our beautiful home. . . . The day we had to leave, I packed as much as I could into the car and just left. I believed that if I got far enough away, I could leave my memories behind and start over. I wanted the boys to continue school, but you can't really live out of your car for long without it showing.
>
> We eventually ended up in a homeless shelter where we found some stability, as well as assistance for me to get the help I needed—first with my health and later with a job. I didn't realize it at the time, but I was severely depressed.
>
> Looking back on that time, I don't know how we pulled through. In addition to helping me with my health and a job, the staff at the shelter also found a place for my sons to attend school. I had no idea that there were schools just for homeless children.

The job didn't pay nearly as much as we needed to live on, so we stayed on at the shelter, then moved to transitional housing. Slowly but surely we got back on our feet.

It seems strange, but living at the shelter really opened my eyes. It was probably the best thing that ever happened to me. It didn't happen overnight, but I've learned to be thankful for the ups and the downs in my life.

It took a few more years for Maxine to be fully independent and live on her own again, but she finally could see the light at the end of the tunnel. Maxine's experience in the shelter made a profound and lasting impact on her. While there, she learned a lot about herself and about what really matters—not money and not things, but family.

From her firsthand experience, she also came to realize that her stereotypes about homeless people were totally unfounded. Almost everyone she met at the shelter—adults and children alike—had the same hopes and dreams as she and her boys. The children wanted to see grandma or grandpa again and play once more with their friends, and they all dreamed of living in their own house again. Maxine learned they also shared some of the same fears—being alone, being so overwhelmed that they wouldn't ever feel normal again.

She also learned that quite a few of the adults had once held decent jobs, but they simply weren't prepared for a sudden, unexpected crisis. Though each person's situation was unique, the drama that unfolded was the same. Like Maxine, they thought that financial disaster happened to other people, not to them.

What moved me the most was that the parents all wanted their kids to go to school. They saw education as the land of opportunity. Mostly, they wanted their kids to succeed in school and go to college so they would have more options than they had.

I'll always be grateful for the other homeless families, and the staff and volunteers who helped me and my boys when we so desperately needed help. The day my sons and I left the shelter and moved into transitional housing, I had two prayers . . . that I would always remember that sense of utter despair I felt during the time that the boys and I were homeless. That is what fuels my work and life now.

My other prayer was that when I got back on my feet again I'd be able to help make life a little better and brighter for homeless families, especially the children. I could see the difference in my own kids when they came back from school each day. This gave me hope for them and for the other children. After I left the shelter and was on my own again, that was my motivation to organize and lead a group of caring people to create Crown Academy, a school that specifically caters to the whole child—the education, social, physical, and spiritual needs of homeless children.

LESSONS LEARNED

Today, because of Maxine's vision for a better life for homeless children and their parents, Crown Academy daily serves the educational, social, physical, and spiritual needs of homeless children in the first through eighth grades. In addition to classroom instruction, the school also provides the children with clothing, toiletries, school supplies, and hot meals. And Maxine recognizes that by reaching out to these underserved and often ignored people in her community, Crown Academy is making a difference in the world.

To prepare for the next *Exercise*, reread Maxine's experience, and as you do, pay particular attention to her recognition and application of the Sacred Promises. Then we will go on to discuss the connection between the promises and Maxine's experience.

EXERCISE

Set aside time when you won't have any distractions, and remember to use your notebook or journal for your notes.

- Maxine says that her primary focus is the Sacred Promise of vision. As you reread Maxine's story, notice the other promises at work in her life. Jot them down in your notebook or journal, and find two or three specific examples of the promises at work in Maxine's life.

In Maxine's experience, all of the Sacred Promises and aspects of world work come into play. Some of the promises, such as **vision** and **gratitude**, stand out more than others because they are evident in what Maxine says. Review the summary in the table to see how these two promises show up in Maxine's own words. And though I have listed in a linear sequence the evidence of the promises at work, this is not the exact order in which Maxine's experience unfolded. Like anyone else's experience would be, hers was anything but sequential and linear! Maxine's experience revealed itself in the same way that life unfolds—in circles and spirals and loops.

Sacred Promise	In Maxine's Own Words
Vision	*At that time, all that mattered were my boys and my memories of my beloved soul mate. . . . It seems strange, but living at the shelter really opened my eyes. . . . the parents all wanted their kids to go to school. They saw education as the land of opportunity.*
Gratitude	*It didn't happen overnight, but I've learned to be thankful for the ups and the downs in my life. . . . I'll always be grateful for the other homeless families, and the staff and volunteers who helped me and my boys when we so desperately needed help.*

Other Sacred Promises, such as **love** and **faith**, are also woven into Maxine's experience. Let's take a closer look at where and how these promises show up for Maxine and what role they play in moving her toward making a meaningful contribution to the world.

Maxine's **love** for her husband is evident, before and after his untimely death. Not only is she passionate about Derrick, Maxine deeply **loves** her twin sons. After her marriage, Maxine and her husband live the "good" life. Their lifestyle reflects her and Derrick's **love** for various kinds of possessions.

As she drove away from her home, Maxine believed that she could leave her painful memories behind and had **faith** that she would end up in a better place. (Notice that the Sacred Promise of vision is also at work here.)

While living at the shelter, Maxine put her **faith** in the shelter staff and volunteers to support her in her recovery process. Ultimately, this creative action led to renewed **faith** in herself.

The shelter staff and volunteers also exhibited **faith** in Maxine, investing their time and energy in supporting her recovery from depression and her sons in continuing their education.

Maxine begins to realize the significance and power of family. After she left the shelter and was on her own again, Maxine was motivated to organize and lead a group of caring people to create Crown Academy, a school that specifically caters to the educational, social, physical, and spiritual needs of homeless children. (Notice that the Sacred Promise of creative action is also at work here.)

My summary list of how the promises show up and are at work in Maxine's experience is just the beginning. As I mentioned earlier, all the promises are in motion for Maxine. A good next step is to review her story and those of others in earlier chapters to get a better sense of the promises at work and their power in shifting the persons involved. Now that the table is prepared, as you complete the next set of *Exercises*, imagine yourself at your own table.

EXERCISES

Set aside time when you won't have any distractions, and remember to use your notebook or journal for your notes.

- Put on your favorite music. Light a candle with the specific intention of sending a little of your own light into the world. Review your notes on the Sacred Promises in Maxine's experience.
- Reflect back on the life you imagined at the beginning of this chapter, where you are aligned with your values and making a meaningful contribution to the world. Using Maxine's experience as a catalyst, describe how the Sacred Promises can help you in *your* journey toward making a meaningful contribution to the world.
- In your notebook or journal, draw two overlapping circles like those in the figure. In one circle, write your name. Beneath your name, list five or six things that you enjoy doing: caring for animals, reading, talking, painting, carpentry, shopping, travel, bicycling, and so on.

(*Continued*)

- Choose three items from the following list, and put them in the other circle:

  - Self
  - Family member
  - Friend
  - Community

  Your circles will look something like this:

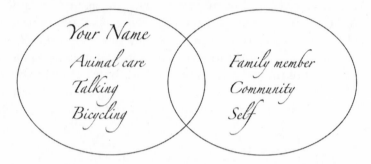

  Your Name
  Animal care
  Talking
  Bicycling

  Family member
  Community
  Self

- For each item in your other circle, list two or three things that might be needed for each category you choose. Then see where what you enjoy matches with a need in the other circle. For example, your library might need books for its annual book drive, and because you love to read, you might have a collection of books to donate. A family member who travels a lot might need someone to look after his or her cat, which matches up with your love of animals.

Congratulations! You have made a number of significant choices—creative actions all—in imagining and claiming the future you desire. Now that you have completed *The Invitation* at the beginning of this chapter and the *Exercises*, take time to celebrate yourself and your accomplishment. You deserve it. Listen to your favorite world music. Visit an area of your city that you've never been to before. Call a friend. Try a new restaurant. Read a book.

In earlier chapters, you were introduced to *Affirmations* to validate your exploration of the Sacred Promises. As you take the next steps to manifest the life you imagine, you will continue to benefit from the affirmations that say, "I'm Doing It!" However, to manifest the future you desire requires you to make a covenant—a sacred commitment—with yourself. The *Promises to Keep* that follow will help you as you dare to wear your soul on the outside and pass your blessings on to others.

PROMISES TO KEEP

I, _____, am committed to being in right relationship with myself, aligned with my values, and making a meaningful contribution to the world. To do so, I will:

- Hold my personal vision so that I do what's necessary to make a meaningful contribution to the world.
- Take positive, life-affirming actions toward the life and world I imagine, so that I will manifest it.
- Commit to nurturing and developing myself, learning from others, and being of use to others.
- Serve until it feels good. And boldly and humbly serve as an instrument of soul.
- Act as a steward on behalf of the future, and pass it on.

- _____

- _____

- _____

Faithfully yours,

_____

The time for the healing of wounds has come. The moment to bridge the chasms that divide us has come. The time to build is upon us.
NELSON MANDELA

CHAPTER 14

The Sacred Promises as a Sacred Life Path

Take good care of the best that is in you.
Self-exploration and personal growth continue
throughout our lifetimes and equip us to tend
to the needs of others.
FREDERIC BRUSSAT AND MARY ANN BRUSSAT

THIS CHAPTER IS A BRIDGE that will connect all that you've learned thus far about the Sacred Promises to how you can use them with intention on your life path, which consists of your calling—your purpose—and your process, or how you live your purpose. Your life path becomes sacred when your intention and commitment to your calling are set apart and infused with love's wide embrace: fierce, uncompromising self-love, love for others, and Divine love.

Just as your calling is uniquely yours, the lessons you will learn on your life path are uniquely yours. At any time along the way, you can practice the spiritual art of pausing, so that you can take a refreshing time out of time to reflect on your direction, what you're learning, or your way of being in the world. Pausing to reflect allows you to step back and become aware of and curious about your process as your life path unfolds.

As I prepared to write this chapter, I found myself doing just that: pausing to savor my life and reflect on my process. Aware that I was creating a bridge between previous chapters and this one, I recognized that I, too, needed a kind of bridge to help me shift from one territory of writing to another. I began looking through the pages of a catalogue that featured a lovely retreat center renowned for its intimate, restorative setting. As I contemplated the sumptuous photographs of this magnificent sanctuary, I transported myself there: inside lush gardens brimming with flowers of every scent and hue, I walk a meandering flagstone path that opens into a welcoming grove of ancient trees. The mossy ground cushions and cradles my feet as whispering cedars beckon me to linger a while.

I clip these and a few more images of garden, forest, and a vast expanse of aquamarine sea. I place them on my writing table in front of me, creating a movable feast for my soul. As I move these seductive images around on my table, I recognize how much I need this sacred pause in my writing process. My soul exhales a long contented sigh and rejoices with an aria of "Amen." I return to my writing, my mind refreshed and my spirit rejuvenated.

We all long for a return to a way of being that has affinity with the soul: appreciating the sun's warm caress on a beautiful summer morning; engaging in the satisfying music of play, joy, magic, and mystery; enjoying right and radiant relationships with ourselves and others; seeing with world vision beyond our differences to embracing our shared humanity; being a citizen of a collective governed by a shared sense of respect and responsibility, guided by a sovereign power older than any culture or civilization, older than time. This Divine force calls us to be an instrument of soul, the force that allows us to lift our eyes to a horizon beyond our day-to-day routine, to fully engage in purposes beyond ourselves, to belong to lives and futures other than our own.

CROSS THE BRIDGE

Saying *yes* to the Sacred Promises as your life path is a radical act not only because it has affinity with soul, but because when you acknowledge and claim your soul, you assert your power and authority in your life. Like any other form of artistry, proclaiming your soul is a political act, a revolutionary offering of bread and water to the hungry and thirsty in spirit. If you want a different tomorrow, you must do something different today. When you say *yes* to the Sacred Promises as your path, this positive, life-affirming action will ensure a different tomorrow.

When you claim the Sacred Promises as yours, you affirm that you have all the resources you need to be on and stay on the path. The key task and challenge of staying on any life path is to acknowledge the boundary between doing and being, so that you can cross the bridge from whatever calls you in the greater world and enter the realm of renewal where your physical and spiritual health and happiness are primary. To make the transition from doing to being, you must cross the threshold from your ordinary everyday life of busyness and service to others and go through the gate to solitude and stillness, to being of service to yourself.

Staying on the path is the invitation that calls you home to yourself so that you will get centered, grounded, and tend to the parts of yourself that have become frazzled or just plain world-weary. And when you gather up the parts of yourself to become whole again, you can reconnect to your calling.

In the exterior world of doing, it is all too easy to lose track of yourself and get out of alignment with your calling. In this world of doing, many distractions conspire against you: old patterns, limiting beliefs, competing priorities, other people's agendas, and your own critical judgments about yourself. The antidote to distraction is getting on and staying on the sacred path, which invites you to an oasis of self-care and self-love. It is a necessary pilgrimage that draws you to the wellspring of Divine love, where you will slake your thirst, drinking in the soul's nectar of beauty, wonder, solitude, silence, humor, and awe.

As you connect what you've learned about the Sacred Promises to keeping the promises you've made to yourself, I invite you to consider how you will use the promises as a blessing on your sacred life path. The wisdom of our great spiritual and faith traditions offers many gifts to support you on your journey. As you travel on your way, the blessings of these spiritual gifts are immeasurable: *intention, commitment, compassion, humility, joy,* and *sanctuary*. And when they are integrated with the Sacred Promises of **gratitude, faith, love, vision, integrity, creative action,** and **legacy**, their power is transformative.

Intention

Of all these spiritual gifts, intention offers you the gift of focus and clarity and is connected to your heart. When your intention is directed beyond yourself and is under the guidance of God or your inner voice, your life will be a blessing to yourself and others, shifting your focus from *me* to *thee* and, ultimately, from *thee* to *we* as a catalyst to transform the lives of countless others. Setting a sacred intention infuses whatever you do with the eloquence and spaciousness of Divine love.

On your sacred life path, your first and most essential task is to set your intention. Seven or eight years ago, Carol first attended one of my retreats where we focused on the Sacred Promises. After attending another such retreat last summer, she told me about the many profound lessons she's learned about the power of intention and how the Sacred Promises continue to inform her path. "Over the years," Carol said, "three promises have made a huge difference in my life: legacy, love, and gratitude."

> Learning about legacy provides continuity to my life. Legacy connects me to the future. Love connects me to the present. Gratitude connects me to my past. I'm focusing my intention on these promises now.

As Carol set her intention on legacy, she gained clarity and insight on what legacy meant to her personally.

> Legacy is the promise that guides me and stays with me. It's what I think about when I'm unclear about what I'm doing or why I'm doing something. It connects me to acting purposefully in the present.

Recently, Carol realized that legacy doesn't mean that she has to go out and conquer the world, create something new, or leave some indelible mark. "Legacy is enough when I live with love and compassion for all things. That's my influence. It's who I am." She now recognizes that living with intention to honor and not harm provides a legacy.

As Carol reflected on the Sacred Promises and her life path, she recognized that intention gave her the focus and specificity she needed to make the promises meaningful to her. Looking back on her first retreat, she recalled that the promises made sense, were very helpful, and provided some very important lessons. Nonetheless, over time the impact of the promises seemed to wane, along with many other good things she experienced.

> Several times in the intervening years, I'd come across my promises notebook or some handwritten note that I'd scrawled someplace, and I'd read and appreciate again some part of my work with the promises.
>   After the retreat this past summer, things are much different now. An internal shift has occurred. This shift is very different from other changes I've experienced. I trace this change to my willingness and readiness to really concentrate on understanding and internalizing what the promises mean to me personally: Carol. Individual. Heart work instead of just head work.

Derived from the Latin *tenere*, which means "to stretch or lean toward," *intention* is about leaning in to something or someone with purpose and resolve, like cornering on your bicycle once the training wheels are taken off. With regard to your intention, you could ask, "How am I leaning in to the promises in my life?" Listening to stories that touch our hearts reminds us of the kind of leaning in we all did as children and now do as adults seeking our own place in the unfolding story of our lives.

Commitment

One of the most important tasks on your life path is commitment. Connected to your heart and your feet, commitment offers you the gift of directed action. Commitment says, "Someone or something is depending on me. Our children are waiting. Our rivers and streams need help. Life is short. Let's get busy." Commitment is the abiding grace that encourages you to put your feet where your heart is. Offering the gifts of significance and urgency, commitment echoes the timeless questions: *If not you, who? If not now, when?* These days, Carol asks herself these questions daily. They keep her focused and shape her priorities.

Although I began the retreat last summer with the intention to extract every drop of experience and learning from it and to use it solely for my own personal growth, I never expected a momentous shift. My only commitment was to having a full experience and being honest; beyond that, I didn't have an agenda. I now realize that the most significant reason for my internal shift was that shift in my commitment. Almost a year later, the result is an integration of the promises into my everyday life, my outlook, and my sense of purpose.

When you asked us to reflect on our own process and pick a word and describe its rhythm, or presence, in our lives, I chose the word *emergence*. But when I started to journal, I didn't write the word *emergence*. I wrote *emergency*. The word surprised me. But it made sense, too. How much time did I have left? And did I really want to continue to live in my comfort zone? Well, I had my answer. The word *emergency*. Try something different and do it, now!

Carol's commitment to herself to fully engage her heart and her feet created the sturdy platform that she needed to step out on faith and begin her bold adventure into the next stage of her life. And her commitment to be honest with herself helped Carol hone her focus from the fuzzy comfort of *emergence* to the beneficial surprise and clarity of *emergency*.

Compassion

Offering the gifts of insight and empathy, compassion is the bounty of your open heart and directed feet combined with the work of your hands. Focused outward, compassion offers the haven of our shared humanity, where we find shelter, understanding, respect, and accord. Turned inward, compassion urges you to set and honor boundaries. As Carol discovered, compassion also offers the sweet ground of self-protection, where you lovingly guard yourself from the would-be saboteurs of moods, thoughts, activities, and people that steal your precious intellectual, emotional, physical, and spiritual energy.

It was the concept of love that actually was the catalyst for my shift in understanding. When we talked about self-love, fiercely dedicated self-love, something clicked. When I practiced loving myself, I saw things in a very different light. I saw myself first as a gifted girl, then as a gifted woman whose passions were buried, denied, and minimized for most of her life. If fierce self-love existed in me, these gifts would be acknowledged, accepted, and utilized. I realized that if I could honor and have compassion for someone else without passing judgment, I could extend the same to myself. I accepted that premise, and found that not only was it a relief, but it freed me to realize that I did want to use my gifts, to see what surfaced in my remaining years.

Humility

As a loving reminder, humility whispers, "It's not about you." To get our attention, sometimes it will shout. Humility invites you to surrender your intentional heart, committed feet, and compassionate hands as a simple act of devotion. It asks us to befriend reverence, bow our head, and surrender our pride and ego. When Carol reflected on her own surrender, she returned to the Sacred Promise of gratitude. "It was the first promise that really challenged me to take a look at my 'stuff.' Gratitude started the whole process of my surrender." Carol carried her parents' genes, the scars of their parenting, and the weight of their negativity: a sense of low self-worth, a knee-jerk response of guilt, and an inability to sort things out in a way that provided for her own self-care. Like so many people, Carol wondered how she could possibly be grateful for parents who had been so utterly indifferent, abusive, and withholding.

Carol said that therapy had helped her piece together her experiences, perceptions, and beliefs into a whole being who understood and accepted that she was not the cause of her parents' misery or their abuse. It also helped her realize that she had choices, that she could be different, that she could change the family legacy. But she still struggled with how to proceed with a new commitment to herself instead of her old reactive and inappropriate choices.

> I began by choosing to thank people who were more removed
> from my direct, day-to-day experience. An important grandmother.
> A primary school teacher. My parents, however, remained at bay.
> I could be grateful for things they had given me, but there was

always a toxic cloud of bilious anger that I had to pass through to
get to the place where I could appreciate them.

Through the years since that first retreat, the Sacred
Promise of gratitude stayed with me. I thought about it often: the
importance of our heritage, remembering and acknowledging it
for *everything* that's occurred. I didn't judge it. I just kept my heart
open to gratitude as a teacher. Oh, what a teacher!

During last summer's retreat, Carol made a bone-deep promise, a covenant with herself. She said, "I will be fully engaged personally, and I will be 100 percent committed to myself. When you
asked who we would 'bring' into the room to honor and express
our thanks to, I was now ready to challenge myself. I was now ready
to bring my parents here, honor them, and bring peace to myself
over my past." Carol humbled herself so that her heart might be
fully open to new life.

Joy

Carol chose to mentally and spiritually bring both her parents
into the room. She creatively imagined them as young and full of
promise and dreams and intentions to succeed in life. Looking
through the lens of joy, Carol invited her mother and father in as
celebrants who truly encouraged her and enjoyed her exploration
into her own life and its purpose. Choosing the radiant attitude
of joy helped Carol reframe her usual reactive thinking about her
parents and freed her to move through and beyond her perceptions and beliefs about her parents and herself.

> Gratitude was and is a deep river of learning. I now recognize it as
> a teacher of my heart and soul. What a blessing! I was getting bored
> with the way I was living my life. I'd never known anything else, but
> I wanted desperately to change. Now that I recognize and know
> what true joy feels like, my commitment to myself is to experience
> it and live joyously for the rest of my life.

Mentally and spiritually bringing her parents into the circle
and acknowledging them in a positive, life-affirming way helped
Carol forgive them. It also helped her forgive herself and allowed
her to break through the walls of her comfort zone into a new

level of responsibility and desire; she made a significant crossing into another realm, another way of being.

As Carol's life path reveals, joy is one of the mightiest gifts of the soul. Joy—the divine alchemy of our open heart, purposeful feet, compassionate hands, and reverently lowered head—offers us the gift of life-giving waters. Not ordinary happiness, but white-water exhilaration. Not ordinary contentment, but profound peace that transcends all understanding.

As Carol's life path continues to unfold, she has set a new intention for herself. "I really want to delve into the additional lessons of gratitude and joy." Through her struggle with honoring her parents, Carol discovered the blessing waters of compassion, forgiveness, and joy. Now, each day she begins by asking herself these questions: "What will emerge from the genuine compassion I now feel for my parents and myself? What pearl? What joy?"

Sanctuary

On our sacred life path, we all need to pause for restoration and renewal. Without pauses, what we call music would be a continuous stream of "white noise." The same holds true in our lives. Without pausing, our lives become a continuous stream of activity. One way to pause is to create a place, moment, or spirit of sanctuary, a sacred garden that feeds your interior life and therefore your exterior life. Sanctuary is also about tempo, about attending to how we live our life and how we travel on our sacred life path. When you pay attention to your life's tempo, the rhythm and pace of your life, you attend to the condition and resonance of your soul.

Sanctuary is not necessarily a literal place, although it may be helpful to begin with a physical place—a room in your home, a corner of your office or desk, a special table. Your place of sanctuary can be indoors or outdoors; a garden, path, porch, or secluded spot in your yard makes an excellent sanctuary. You can find sanctuary in a haven that awakens your senses, a haven of color and texture, a place vibrant with tranquility: flowers and trees, stones and grasses, butterflies and birds. A place with the fragrance and sounds of life, children playing, elders conversing about the news of the day, a river rushing headlong to join the sea.

Whether it's a physical or an internal place, sanctuary is an essential resource on your sacred life path, a place of retreat, refuge, and repose. Sanctuary offers the gifts of refreshment and rejuvenation, a place to reconnect with your creativity. It is a place to listen, to lean in to what gives you joy, what restores your vitality. A place of deep nourishment, sanctuary provides you with food for your soul.

When we take time to slow down, quiet ourselves, and reflect on our lives—to renew ourselves and our commitments—important changes happen, within and without. As we are renewed as parents, teachers, counselors, clergy, attorneys, and community leaders, we in turn contribute to the renewal of our families, workplaces, schools, professions, communities, and world.

Whatever you imagine it to be, set an intention to create sanctuary. When you do so, you commit to nurturing yourself, to tuning in to the voices that affirm, heal, celebrate, and rejoice in you. Ultimately, sanctuary will become a state of consciousness, a way of being. The twin goals of sanctuary are to create for yourself a refuge wherever you are with whatever you have, a refuge where renewal and sustenance are central. In *Seasons of Grace*, Alan Jones writes, "A woman friend with a chronic illness uses her waiting time in the doctor's office to write small poems and songs to fight off the bad vibes."

Sanctuary speaks the language of the soul. Sanctuary adores the blessings of silence, particularly the spaciousness of what Mother Teresa calls the silence of the heart. In this necessary silence, she writes, "you can hear God everywhere—in the closing of the door, in the person who needs you, in the birds that sing, in the flowers, in the animals." Sanctuary delights in the treasure of solitude, for that is the chalice from which the soul drinks. Sanctuary rejoices at the altar of poetry and music, amazes on the shores of mystery and awe, sings through the currents of conversation, merriment, and surprise, communes with the refugee or pilgrim inside and outside of ourselves.

Author and social artist Margaret Walker says, "A writer needs certain conditions in which to work and create art." She envisioned sanctuary as "a piece of time; a peace of mind; a quiet place." Virginia Woolf imagined sanctuary as "a room of one's own," a private, protected place where she had quiet time, alone time, soul time, creative time.

Carol's vision of sanctuary is to have a "room" of her own. She already has a comfortable cabin deep in the heart of a majestic old-growth forest. But it isn't a sanctuary in Carol's mind. "Not yet," she says. "At the moment, my cabin is possessed by my possessions, and so am I." Going forward, Carol is setting her intention to re-create her cabin into a physical and spiritual sanctuary.

> This means I must rid myself of my thousands of objects. No exaggeration here. When I returned home after the last retreat, I counted the pieces of pottery, porcelain, glassware, and miscellaneous objects on my seven-foot counter over the kitchen sink: over one hundred items, not including the notepaper, pencils, pens, keys, and small tools that I have there because they're useful. So much love in and for all these things. They've been a substitute for authentic love, real relationships. I can see that now.

Knowing that love is the only thing that multiplies when we give it away freely and joyously, Carol has spent the last several months freeing herself of her many possessions. She sold a few items, but gave most away—freely and joyously. And as she freed herself of her many possessions, she recognized that sanctuary was in the surrender of the old way for the new way. Carol now finds sanctuary in her cabin and in herself.

ART AND SOUL

It's been almost a year since her summer retreat. This time around, Carol truly realized that life is precious and, in the grand design of creation, life is short. "These days, I just want to keep it real. It's been eight months since the retreat. So much of what I experienced still informs my day. I don't know if I go more than a day without checking in with what one of the promises means to me and can teach me on my sacred life path."

When I asked Carol if she had any advice for fellow travelers on their journeys, she said, "Don't take so long to get it. Don't take as long as I did to jump into the waters of joy. At sixty-five years of age, I can say that. Life really goes by quickly, especially if you're raising children, earning a living, and just living your life doing the best you can with what you've been given. Don't just be a tourist in your own life. Be a resident. Be engaged. Be intentional. Be committed."

And I would add, be clear about your calling and your values. If you are, your life's journey will be easier, because every choice you make will be driven and organized by your calling and your values.

In *The Mission of Art*, Alex Grey discusses the significance of the artist's calling. When an artist lives with intention and follows her calling, through her art she becomes a channel for spiritual power, and her "labors of heart and soul become batteries of transcendental energy." In other words, spiritual power flows from the Divine through the artist into her art, and from her art into the receiver. Just as the artist is transformed by this holy transfer of power, the receiver is also transformed by the artist's art.

When we dare to wear our souls on the outside, we say *yes* to our artistry, for on our sacred life path each of us is called to be a social artist in our interactions at home, work, and beyond. When you say *yes* to your artistry, you open yourself to a transformative infusion of spiritual power. And the labors of your heart and soul will become a transcendental force, a powerful energy that transforms those around you with the radiance of your love and light.

RESOURCES FOR YOUR JOURNEY

Set aside time when you won't have any distractions, and remember to use your notebook or journal for your notes.

- Create a moment of sanctuary: put on your favorite soothing music, and light a candle or incense. As you look ahead on your sacred life path, set a specific intention for the next step you will take, which will be to write and tell your own story. For example, your intention might be to express gratitude every day, to encourage you as you wear your soul on the outside. It might be to create an indoor or outdoor space that honors your sacred life path.
- Create a collage that will help you cross the bridge from wherever you are now to prepare to write and tell your own story. You may recall the collage I mentioned earlier in this chapter, which helped me make the transition from writing the previous chapter to writing this chapter.

- Create your own list of *Affirmations*—positive, supportive statements that will encourage and inspire you as you continue your journey on your sacred life path. Include at least one affirmation for each of the spiritual gifts on your path: *intention, commitment, compassion, humility, joy,* and *sanctuary.* Your affirmations will provide spiritual bread for your journey. For the next thirty days, read your affirmations aloud at least twice a day. Read them in the morning to frame your day and feed your day dreams, and again in the evening to seed your night dreams. As part of your spiritual practice, make a copy and put it in your wallet or purse. Refer to your affirmations when you need encouragement and refreshment.

> *In solitude, we are silent, so that we may hear,*
> *focused so that we may craft substantial things.*
> PAM GROUT

CHAPTER 15

I Dared . . . I'm Doing It

Stories are medicine, small doses of what matters,
and it is the telling that releases the medicine, the
telling that soothes our pain and shares our joy.
MARK NEPO

IN KISWAHILI, *HABARI GANI* MEANS "What's the news?" or "What's happening now?" In these next pages, you will read small doses of what's happening now, of what matters in the lives of ordinary people, including two individuals you met earlier—Vera and my father, Earnest McEwen Jr. The stories and songs on these pages breathe the timeless, universal truths of the Seven Sacred Promises, truths that mentor us in ways of being that are older than time, truths that breathe just beneath the surface of our ever busy lives. Each story begins with a small dose of what matters, a motif from my poem "Song to Myself."

All the people here are just like you and me. We all care. We care about ourselves. We care about one another. We want to leave the world a little bit better off than the way we found it. As stewards of the future, we dare to wear our souls on the outside to be right with ourselves and with others. As instruments of soul, we sound the way for others in our immediate circles, and beyond.

You are a magnificent story. You are painting on the canvas of your soul. And at the end of this chapter, you will give voice to your story, responding to the question "*Habari gani?* What's happening now?" by drawing from the deep wellspring and transformative power of your own true voice.

Until then, I trust that you will be moved by these stories of hope, radiance, and celebration. And as you encounter each individual soul, I trust that you will feel the sweet shimmer of your own story and hear the resonance of your own true voice. I trust that you will bask in the joy and inspiration of the storytellers, allowing them to illuminate your sacred life path. Accept the gifts they offer so that you can pass these stories on and faithfully light the path for others.

So now, I invite you to get cozy, sip a cup of tea or your favorite coffee, and join me by the fire to hear the good news.

> It doesn't matter to me
> what you do or where you work.
> I want to know
> who you are
> when the sun goes down
> and if you are willing
> to put everything on the line
> to fulfill your soul's desire.

Vera

In Chapter Two, you met Vera at the divine union of her calling and passion. It's been almost a year since she began homeschooling her daughter and launched her private practice as a cranial-sacral therapist. The seeds she has sown through her daily acts of service, expressed through gratitude, faith, love, and the other Sacred Promises, are now providing a harvest of blessings for Vera, her daughter, as well as her family, clients, community, and the world beyond.

When she started her private practice about a year ago, Vera's personal vision was to begin as a solo practitioner and then, over the next few years, build a "wellness community," an ensemble of like-hearted practitioners. "I want to work with other therapists, as well as doctors, neurosurgeons, nutritionists, and other professionals who care deeply about health and well-being and who really understand that we are designed by God's grace to move toward wholeness, toward health. In a few years, that's where I see myself."

I spoke with Vera recently to hear about what's happening now on her journey. "*Habari gani,* Vera. What's the news?" As usual, she was beaming with joy.

This past year has been amazing! It's been a steady stream of miracles, one right after another.

This time last year, I was dreaming of building a wellness community. Well, today I'm doing it! It's all happening so fast. Don't get me wrong, though. It didn't happen overnight, and I believe that it wouldn't have happened at all if I hadn't been intentional and 100 percent committed to my calling and life path. I have learned the power of gratitude BIG TIME . . . and the power of faith, vision, and all the other promises. I've continued to write my client thank-you notes, my notes of gratitude. My clients are now referring family members and friends; I'm treating people of all ages. This time last year, I was praying about how to find clients. Now, most days, I'm fully booked.

To better accommodate the needs of individual clients and to support her vision of building a wellness community, Vera told me of the difficult decision she made to move her office to a different location.

A few months before my lease was up, I knew I had to move to a new location. I'm not sure exactly how or when I knew. It was kind of like when I knew I had to leave my engineering job and open my practice and homeschool.

Well, when the building owner approached me about my current lease, I thought, what do I say? That I know I have to leave?! I knew I needed to be honest with him, so I told him about my vision for expanding my practice and creating a wellness community. He said, "No problem. Come see my other building. I want to keep you as a tenant." You know me. I jumped for joy and sang, "Bonus!" When I saw the offices on the first level, I thought, mmm . . . nice. The "top of the world" offices on the second level were magnificent but just didn't feel right. When I saw the office space at the basement level, I knew for an absolute fact that it was

the space God intended us to have; He planned it long before
I arrived.

There are a series of offices with a central space for reception.
The offices used to be a counseling facility, so there is extra
insulation in the walls for privacy. There is a bathroom right next
to Adrianna's homeschool room; it's private, so I don't have to
worry about her safety. Better location. Plenty of free parking. And,
there are plenty of rooms for expansion and growth—space for my
wellness community practitioners! It's perfect. And the building
owner is holding the unoccupied offices for me rent-free until
they fill.

Well, things took off from there so rapidly that I know it's
Divine.

Vera then told me about another waterfall of unexpected blessings. The carpenter who custom-built the office and homeschool
bookshelves for her old office disassembled and then reconfig-
ured them for her new space—for free. An acquaintance offered
Vera all the interior paint she needed for twenty-five dollars, and a
group of the carpenter's friends painted her entire suite of offices
in exchange for Vera's donation to a needy charity.

Here's the part of Vera's story that allows us to see why she's so
enthusiastic about and grateful that she responded to her calling
to become a cranial-sacral healer.

A five-year-old boy named Lucas [not his real name] came to my
office this week for a treatment. He has a feeding tube because
he won't eat. His speech and social skills are at a level below
what they should be for his age. I think he has experienced some
deep trauma, perhaps abuse, and most likely some psychological
damage. His grandmother brought Lucas to my office. After talking
with her about Lucas's challenges, including his unwillingness to be
touched by anyone, I just said flat out, "I'm expecting a God-sized
miracle."

So that I could treat him, I asked Lucas if it was OK for me to
touch him. He immediately backed away from me and said, "No,
no, time to go home, time to go home." I told him that I didn't
need to touch him, and he seemed to calm down a little.

I had brought a toy train and Lincoln Logs for him to play
with, so we both sat on the floor and played with the toys, though
Lucas always made sure he was close to the door. Finally, I just laid

back on the floor—and he came right to me! He snuggled with me, let me touch him, which led to my being able to treat him. It was probably the most significant treatment I've ever done. The treatment was so calming that Lucas was sleepy at the end. But when he stood up, he started dancing!

In addition to the children, I like to treat the mothers or other care providers so they can do some of this work for their children's sake outside the office. Guess what! Lucas's grandmother is coming for her first treatment on Monday!

Vera's miracles keep flowing from the deep wellspring of her saying *yes* to God's legacy for her. For Vera, wearing her soul on the outside is as natural as breathing, for she is simply robed in the garment of her calling and signature presence. "You know what makes all of this so worthwhile is the difference I see in my own daughter. A little over a year ago, I overheard Adrianna playing with her Barbie dolls. In her imaginary conversation, Barbie said to one of her girlfriend dolls, 'I'm busy. I can't go out tonight. I've gotta take a conference call.' That grabbed me by my heartstrings."

These days, between every client, Adrianna and Vera are together. They're either engaged in their homeschooling adventures or just hanging out. "We always have lunch together. Sometimes we take a field trip as part of our lunch. We sing, tell stories, and by helping Adrianna with her language lessons, I'm learning what she's learning. I'm in seventh heaven! And Adrianna, well, she couldn't be happier." Vera said that just last week, Adrianna researched and wrote a report for her lesson on international world culture. She described a wonderful creativity school in Italy. Their motto is "Nothing without joy!" And then Adrianna said, "Hey, Mom, that sounds like a good motto for our school, too."

I want to know
   if you can look into the eyes
   of the young woman
   who sleeps with fear each night

the one who dared to walk
away from the hands that pummeled her.
I want to know
if you can share her pain.

Jean

For the past six years, Jean has devoted herself to developing the necessary skills, character qualities, and spiritual practices to become a hospice professional. Her dream is to coach and train other hospice workers, and to start her own business dedicated to their personal, professional, and spiritual development.

Jean sailed through her six years of training and confidently worked for several years as a hospice professional for a large health care network. However, when she began to seriously consider launching her own business, she froze, immobilized by her chorus of inner critics. Recognizing that she was stuck and unable to move forward with her personal vision, Jean sought coaching for herself.

Together we created a plan for Jean to delve more deeply into the Sacred Promises and her sacred life path, focusing primarily on gratitude and sanctuary. Jean's task was to disengage her chorus of critics and escort them once and for all out of her life. In addition to other spiritual resources, Jean committed to a gratitude practice that included appreciation, compassion, and forgiveness. "In my practice of gratitude, I learned that appreciation, compassion, and forgiveness have presence. Each has a shape, texture, weight, and color, which continues to instruct and guide me."

Jean's courageous and loving confrontation of her inner critics led to a significant breakthrough. "This was some of the most difficult, yet joyous work I've ever done." To bring closure to her reparation and forgiveness work, Jean created a ceremony of gratitude to honor her past, reinvigorate her present, and celebrate her newfound freedom to move boldly toward her dream.

Tonight I create a ceremony to burn the hateful, negative words of the choir of my mind. I bring forward anyone who has a voice in this choir. One by one, I honor, lovingly thank, and let go of the voices that don't serve to lift me up. As I let go of each voice, I pick up a small slip of paper with that person's name on it, my painful memory associated with him or her, and a positive affirmation to replace the negative, painful memory. Then I burn the piece of paper in a special vessel, my Burning Bowl.

With each piece of burning paper, I release the pain, sadness, hurt, and anger from my spirit and from the cells of my body. With each piece of burning paper, I turn off the volume of a hurtful voice and turn up the voice of my capable, strong, resilient self. With each piece of burning paper, I say these words: "In reverence and love I thank you for your presence in my life. You didn't intend to hurt the soul of my child, but she was injured; she carries your words with her. I know that I'm blessed by the good and the bad. And I pray that the blessings of gratitude will continue to be revealed. Now, I return you into the ground of your life, lived by you. As of today, I am free of your judgments and grief. I am free of the burden within my soul." I imagine myself putting a rose over the heart and in the hands of my beloveds.

After the flame shrinks to a faint glow, I stand in my dimly lit room, and I allow my soul to radiate outward for all to see. I am free from the voices of pain, sadness, hurt, and anger. I am free to believe in my goodness, my abilities, and my connection to God. All is deep. All is mine. As my spirit heals, I can shine! I will open to the healing of others. I am a beacon of light into this world.

During the past few months, Jean has continued to be blessed by new insights. As her journey unfolds, she has learned that new roses will indeed grow from her old wounds, for she perceives their opening buds in the questions she's living at the moment: *What reward did I receive from the messages I chose to keep with me all these years? Do I want that reward to control my life now? What spiritual practice will I follow instead?* As Jean enriches her learning about gratitude, she revels in the rich harmonies of appreciation, compassion, and forgiveness.

These past few months, I have been very silent inside, sitting with God in patience and wonder. I am beginning to understand what others see in me—a person with a huge heart, full of love for others. And growing in love for myself. May I continue on this sacred path until I can feel that same respect and love for myself as I have for others and to feel it with ease and grace. May I continue to enjoy the full measure of this sanctuary of silence within my soul. May I continue to celebrate the Spirit of God within me and feel love's holy light within my soul.

Shortly after her gratitude ceremony, Jean composed this praise poem to celebrate herself, and the healing power of gratitude and sanctuary.

I celebrate
I celebrate the Spirit of God within me
My voice sings loud
My voice sings true
My voice sings of me
I celebrate
I celebrate the Spirit of God within me
I feel the light within my soul
I feel the voice of me
I celebrate
I celebrate the Spirit of God within me
I am what I was created for
I am the woman I am
I am a woman of size
I am ego free
I celebrate
I celebrate the Spirit of God within me
I am free
I am free of the voices within me
There is only room for me
I celebrate
I celebrate the Spirit of God within me

I want to know
    if you will throw away your cloak
    and show your heart if you will dare
    to wear your soul on the outside.

Eliza

When my friend Eliza was diagnosed with breast cancer, she was shocked, but not devastated. A warm, outgoing, take-charge kind of person, her luminous spirit has been evident throughout her journey with cancer. Shortly after her diagnosis, and long before she began radiation therapy, Eliza began visualizing the X-rays flowing into her body as healing waves of energy. These redemptive agents of hope and light she named Radiant Beams! And to stay connected with her family and many friends, Eliza created a newsletter to tell the story about her journey with cancer.

> I'm celebrating the conclusion of this portion of my journey with cancer by going to Georgia to visit my son Greg. I'm leaving on October 4, and will be gone for five days. I can't wait! Greg is taking me to the Georgia National Fair in Perry, Georgia. Wherever that is. There will no doubt be some wonderful Southern food. Life is good.

Whether she had good news or not-so-good good news to share in her newsletter, Eliza always included a simple note of thanksgiving and inspiration.

> I cannot believe it's been almost a year since I encountered cancer. I found the lump Halloween weekend, was diagnosed in November, had surgery in December, then for six weeks in January encountered Radiant Beams, then finally was infused with chemo drugs for six months. Whew. It has been some journey.
>
> I am looking forward to new and different things this coming year. Once again, my thanks to all of you who have been so supportive throughout this enlightening experience. Your cards, words of encouragement, and prayers have meant more to me than you can know. I count myself blessed to have so many wonderful and caring friends.
>
> Here's a thought for the day: When a mighty ship is moored in the harbor, it is safe. But mighty ships were not built to remain in the harbor.

It doesn't matter to me
     how many mountains
     you've climbed or will climb.
I want to know
     if you've fallen down
     in the valley of despair.

> I want to know
>   if you've scarred your knees
>   on the stones of self-abandonment.
> I want to know
>   how long you've been hidden in the shadows
>   of hypocrisy prejudice addiction abuse.
> I want to know
>   if you will stop
>   to light a candle and pray with others
>   who will surely wander there.

Tamra

Unfortunately, the word *addict* conjures up a negative image in most people's minds: a person of immoral character, without value to society, who deliberately chooses to engage in destructive behavior. In reality, individuals who are considered addicts are just like you and me. Just like Tamra.

Five years ago, Tamra was arrested for "disturbing the peace." She is grateful to the prosecutors who offered her a deferred sentence on the condition that she obtain treatment for her addiction, get substance abuse and behavioral counseling, and stay out of trouble with the law. Tamra knows she was one of the lucky ones. But she also says that what her prosecutors did for her should be the norm, not the exception.

> I used to call myself an addict. But not anymore. I now realize that I'm a human being with an illness called addiction. That's a lot different than saying I'm an addict, which sounds like I'm a bad person, or I have a character defect or something worse. I'm a good person. I just got mixed up with the wrong crowd and the wrong pills.

As Tamra's prosecutors and judge realized, individuals with addictions cannot be cured through incarceration. However, their addictions can be treated with counseling, mentoring, and in some cases medication. Through education and mentoring, these individuals can change their behaviors as well, which will contribute to significant changes in lifestyle.

We don't often hear stories about people like Tamra who have changed their values and behaviors, who live productive, meaningful lives, and who are making a better life for themselves and their community. But for every story like Tamra's there are thousands more. If anyone were to ask Tamra the question *"Habari gani?"* she would declare, "I'm glad I got a second chance. Not everybody does. So I'm doing this for my son Tyler and for all those other people who are just like me but maybe weren't so lucky."

Driven to help others as she was helped, Tamra is determined to change her story, which will change her family's story, and it will change the legacy she's creating for her son. It took some time for Tamra to obtain joint custody of her son, but she now has it, and she's established a stable, loving home for Tyler.

She works part time for the Maricopa County Juvenile Court's Positive Parenting Program, through which parents help other parents overcome the hurdles that can lead to their children's becoming wards of the state. During the past three years, Tamra attended Mesa Community College and earned her associate's degree. She is currently attending Arizona State University and working on her degree in social work. After that, she plans to go to law school, because she knows what kind of impact a prosecutor or judge has over a person's life.

Tamra also volunteers with the city, helping people who are former substance abusers to connect with the myriad services designed to help create stable families and safer communities, such as substance-abuse counseling, G.E.D. testing, job-skills training, and higher education. Tamra also helps these individuals learn positive life skills. "We use a curriculum that focuses on strengths, that promotes positive, uplifting values and new ways of thinking and acting."

Each day she thanks her lucky stars that she's able to give back something to individuals who are pretty much like her, doing the best they can with what they have to give their kids a better life. Tamra knows that even though they may not get a lucky break like she did, they still deserve a second chance.

I am thankful to be raising Tyler in a loving, caring home— something I never knew. I also want to help and inspire others who have fallen through the cracks to find the stability, peace of mind, and hope that I have found. I want them to know that they, too, can change and lead a productive life filled with purpose and promise.

I want to know
 if you will take the time to be still
 call the names and pass the cup
 to honor the ancestors
 who cleared a path
 and broke new ground
 for you and your children.

Lionel

A few years ago, I invited my clients to express their thanks for the power and blessings of the Sacred Promises in their lives. Lionel is a senior manager for a large, urban trauma hospital. Typically, I see him every few years, mostly when he's attending courses that I teach at the university that is affiliated with the trauma center.

As I struggle with life as a single father and manager of a challenging department at the Medical Center, I have found that the best way to parent and lead is to make sure my own compass is pointed in the right direction. No one can do it alone, and I'm no exception. I have family and friends, priests, authors like Thomas Merton, Simone Weil, Dorothy Day, and others to help me on the journey. I've added your voice to that list of guides.

My job is challenging. I deal with difficult issues in a trauma hospital setting and life doesn't get more real and challenging than that. Being a single dad is also challenging and my number one focus. I have a great relationship with my 14-year old son, but to keep it going that way means I have to know and keep checking the direction of that inner compass again. To do any of this well means being real.

I see people from all walks of life every day and there's no time to think sometimes, only to react. To be able to react in line with one's beliefs means you've got to be in tune with those beliefs so they are a natural part of you. I've attended several seminars you've led through the university these past many years. I have to tell you that I'm not normally big on seminars, and find many of them to be wasted time with too much emphasis on feel good platitudes that have nothing to do with the reality of everyday life. From the first seminar of yours I attended, I found you to be strikingly different. You are honest and shared different pains you've faced growing up and moving through your life's journey. You share your courage, determination, laughter, warmth, encouragement, and spirit with us. For that I thank you.

Your talks help me to dig deeper, to refocus my efforts . . . much like a lighthouse can guide a ship. My attending your classes has been like cruising past the lighthouse to take a reading, perhaps get some new information so I can head back out to sea and brave the elements. I don't know if I could ask much more than that from anybody.

Thanks, Gloria, for being there and sharing. You really mean a lot to me, and I'm so glad you are there. And thanks for giving me time to reflect on some things I am grateful for, too.

It doesn't matter to me
   how much bread you can afford
   to put on your own table.
I want to know
   if you will knead and wait
   and bake the bread and share
   your blessings at someone else's table.

Darlene

After divorcing her husband, Darlene moved into a small trailer home with her two young sons. Christmas was fast approaching, but she had no extra money. As she stared at the floor of her tiny living room, she thought, "This will definitely be a year without presents for my boys." She could give them her love, and that was all. Knowing that they were too young to understand that love is what Christmas should be all about, she also knew that they were going to have to learn. Little did Darlene know that her sons would learn about love and a whole lot more.

On Christmas Eve, we had a record snowfall. My boys went outside
to shovel our walkway and driveway—to keep up with the quickly
falling snow. As evening came, they went next door and helped our
elderly neighbor Jim shovel his driveway. When they came inside,
I suggested we sing Christmas carols and then each of us would
tell a story about our best-ever Christmas. We had a good time just
being together. Neither of my sons asked me why we didn't have
a tree this year. That night, when I was sure my sons were sound
asleep, I sat on the couch in our tiny living room and just wept.
I cried for me. I cried for my sons. I even cried for my ex-husband.
Sometimes I cried tears of sadness. Sometimes I wept for joy.
I finally went to bed and cried myself to sleep.

The next morning on Christmas day, I got up bright and
early. I peered outside and saw that the snowstorm had passed.
The sky was a bright, bright blue and everywhere you looked
snow—white, sparkling, new-fallen snow. "The boys would love to
make snow angels," I thought. They both loved to be the first
to make footprints in the fresh snow, and they loved making snow
angels. Sometimes they'd lay down head-to-head in the snow and
make a double angel.

I don't know why, but I opened the door of our trailer to check
our mailbox. No one, not even the mail truck could have made
it through all that snow, but I checked it anyway. To my surprise,
there was a note inside. My boys had told our neighbor Jim that
Santa Claus wouldn't be visiting our house this year because we
had no money. I turned the note over and taped to the back was a
crisp, clean fifty-dollar bill. Jim had given me enough money to buy
the boys what they wanted—new baseball mitts. In addition, there
was enough left over to restock the basic groceries we needed. Jim's
only request was that when I was able to do so, that I help others
as he helped us.

That morning when my sons got up, I told them about the
fifty dollars Jim had given us for their Christmas gifts. They looked
at each other with surprise and glee, then abruptly stopped their
celebration as they realized the significance of Jim's gift. You see,
Jim wasn't well off either. As a matter of fact, the utility company
had shut his power off once already that winter because he
couldn't pay his bill.

The boys quickly put on their coats to go next door to thank
Jim for his generous gift. But they stopped short when they opened
the trailer door and saw a perfectly formed adult-sized snow angel
right in front of our steps. The snow angel surprised them. But
there were absolutely no footprints in the snow. Just the angel.

We never did find out who made the snow angel; Jim said there was no way that he could or would get down in the snow and flap his arms and legs like that. But we know an angel brought us quite a blessing that Christmas.

Jim passed away the following spring. My boys and I still think about that special Christmas and how Jim gave without asking for anything in return, just that we help others as he helped us. We've made a point of doing just that, and we have faith that we're touching others' lives like Jim touched ours.

It doesn't matter to me
   that you have a past.
I want to know
   if you will celebrate your present
   if you will take a stand
   declare yourself sing *I am*
   boldly and with rejoicing
   not only to the stars at night
   but to anyone
   anywhere
   without apologies
   or regrets.

Earnest

Devoted to lifelong self-improvement and to education in general, my father lived his life reaching out to others who desired a strong educational foundation, fulfilling his promise to Mr. Faulkner to "pass it on." My father was a man with passionate intention and, in so many ways, a visionary who was far ahead of the era in which he lived.

At Alcorn A&M College, my father reaped the rich rewards of student life. And in June 1957, four years after he began college, he graduated with distinction. To his credit as well as deep sorrow, he graduated not from his beloved Alcorn but from Central State College in Wilberforce, Ohio. As you know from the story of his youth, my father was always very clear about and committed to his values. Among his rock solid values was respect for all others—no matter what. A natural leader, my father became president of the

Alcorn Student Council during a period of great turbulence and racial unrest.

In March 1957, just three months before he was due to gradu-ate from Alcorn, my father took a stand against racial injustice both in his role as student council president and as a champion for civil rights. And for this, he and a handful of other student leaders were expelled, or "ousted," as they called it during those tense, horrible years leading up to what we now call the civil rights move-ment. Knowing that his lifelong dream could be in jeopardy, if not his life, he was willing to give it all up for what he believed was a moral and spiritual imperative. My sixth grade teacher, Ms. Mary Jane Gillespie, used to say, "Character is forged not when the sea is smooth as glass, but in the gale-tossed riot of the roiling sea."

Habari gani?

A few months ago, one of my sisters met Dr. Joy Williamson, a professor of the history of education. Upon hearing my sister's last name, McEwen, the professor asked, "Do you happen to know an Earnest McEwen Jr.? I'd sure like to meet him. I just published a book about the role of students in black colleges as a force for change within the black freedom struggle in Mississippi. As stu-dent body president at Alcorn, Mr. McEwen left an indelible legacy of courage and integrity."

Habari gani indeed.

Through Dr. Williamson's scholarship and long stride of spirit, my family is now learning about events in my father's life that we never knew. With gratitude and hope, I thank Dr. Williamson for her important contribution to this relatively impoverished field of study. I thank my sister Doris for allowing God to order her steps on her life path, for if she had not heeded His call in her current work, who knows when or if her path and Dr. Williamson's would have crossed. I trust that as my father's legacy continues to be revealed, it will be a blessing, a gentle rain, another small dose of what matters, another cup of fierce possibility.

GIVE VOICE TO YOUR STORY

We have come full circle. The lives of the people you've met here in this chapter and throughout the book will continue to unfold, just as your life and your great story will continue to be revealed.

And as they do, I invite you to consider story as instrument, story as bell.

In cultures throughout the world, bells symbolize calling. The soft or loud chimes of our clocks call to awaken us with the dawn. Chimes and bells are a call to meditation, contemplation, and prayer. In many places, in the town square or city center, the great bells of the carillon call out the time every hour on the hour. And in our diverse sanctuaries of learning, bells call us to our lessons, to whatever we must learn or remember or forget. Then they call us to gather ourselves and move our feet from one sanctuary of learning to another.

Now you have an opportunity to ring your bell, to hear the unique sound of your own story, in your own true voice. As you prepare to take the next step on your journey, I invite you to remember the Sacred Promises, to remember your signature presence, and remember your calling. As well, remember how your heart responded, how your soul shimmered as you tuned into the news of other people, other bells chiming their stories. And remember that when a bell rings, it invites a resounding, an echo that repeats the sound of your soul's singing, your soul's calling out. When other instruments, other people, hear your story they will pick up on the sound of it, on whatever vibe you are sending out into the world.

Your bell matters. So take good care of your soul. Be a faithful steward of your story. For others who tune into it will carry it back out into the world. As you prepare to give voice to your story, ask yourself, what story am I ringing? What story am I sending out into the world? Is mine a story of gratitude, a story of faith? Is mine a story of light and celebration? Is mine a story lit with joy? In the great story of my life, am I ringing out the sounds of kindness and love and hope and inspiration?

TELLING YOUR STORY

Set aside time when you won't have any distractions, and remember to use your notebook or journal for your notes.

(Continued)

The purpose of telling your story is to better understand your-self. When you're living your life, you don't necessarily slow down and pay attention to the story that you call daily life. Telling your story is also about listening, deep listening, which is a way to honor, value, and recognize how your story—your life—is unfolding as you live your legacy now. Telling and listening to your story will help make the invisible currents of your life visible, so that you can become more conscious of your choices. Telling and listening to your story will inform and transform your life.

- As you reflect on your life path thus far, ask yourself, "*Habari gani?* What's the news? What's happening now in the great story of your life?" As you consider the news of your life, remember that you already have lots of material to work with from all of the *Exercises, Affirmations,* and *Questions for Reflection* you've encountered throughout this book. They are a resource to you. Use them to inform your story.

- *What do you imagine you are? What do you hope to become? What do you want to call out?* Author Rami Shapiro reminds us that "the stories we tell ourselves about ourselves determine the quality of the selves we imagine we are. What we imagine we are, we call out and that is what we become." These questions echo back to the questions we've encountered throughout this book, for they are at once the larger and very intimate questions that give shape, texture, and resonance to your life, including questions such as these:

  - *What matters to me?*
  - *What do I stand for?*
  - *What do I want to create and for whom?*
  - *How will I inhabit my life so that I live in harmony with my values?*
  - *What will I create of enduring value to pass on to others?*

To begin to give voice to your story, I invite you to ease into the realm of sanctuary: put on your favorite soothing music, light a candle, and visualize the person or persons whom you want to hear your story—yourself, a loved one, a favorite friend or other teacher. If you have a photo of that person, put it in a place where you can easily see it.

While I was sounding out and writing the early chapters of this book, I kept an old photograph of my father on my writing table. In this photo, he's eleven or twelve years old. His eyes look straight into the camera. His heart looks deep into the eye and soul of the world. My father is dressed in his Sunday best. A borrowed hand-me-down hat crowns his head. Several sizes too large, it salutes the future, its wide brim slanted just this side of center. His too-small jacket is buttoned askew, and the too-long sleeves of his shirt frame his long and elegant hands. Next to this photo is one of my mother and father—married, grateful parents of five daughters, and several grandchildren. Next to this, a photo of my daughter, practically full grown.

These photos of my parents and daughter helped me focus on my unfolding story of legacy, providing a little extra spark of inspiration when I needed it. Each photo offered an emotional connection to why I was writing the book, to why I was telling my story, to listening that informed me and my process.

- In your notebook, journal, or on another sheet of paper, draw seven circles. Draw them so that they are separate, not overlapping. In each circle, write in one of the Seven Sacred Promises. Now, ask yourself, "Which promise is calling to me? Legacy, integrity, love, or another promise?" The promise that calls to you now is where you'll begin to write your story, because the promise that calls to you now is the area of your life that is already sounding. It's already speaking in a language and voice that you can hear. This is the promise that is calling your name, so to speak. In my workshops, there's always someone who says, "Well, I really can't choose just one. Now what?" It's OK to choose more than one, if that's really true for you. But complete your promise circles one after the other, so that you can give each one your undivided attention.

(*Continued*)

- On another blank sheet of paper, draw one big circle and write the promise you chose inside it. Now, just listen. Listen closely and respectfully. What is this Sacred Promise whispering, saying, singing to you? Whatever it tells you, write it down or draw it or make a collage of it.

- This listening and receiving may take awhile. Give yourself plenty of time—at least an hour. When you are done, read this part of your story aloud. Reading your story silently has its place. Reading it aloud at this stage of your journey will add to your story the breath of your life, the sound of your voice, the music of your soul. Reading it aloud will also reveal other aspects of your story that will only surface when you add breath and sound. If you made a drawing or a collage, you "read" the drawing or collage by talking about the picture or the images as if you were talking about it to that special someone you identified earlier.

    Remember that the most important circle is the one that calls to you right now, the one that gives voice to what is right in front of you.

- You will repeat this process for each of the Sacred Promises. You can complete a promise a day or week or month. There is no great rush. And soul will not be rushed anyway.

- What is your story saying to you? What is it whispering or singing? Listen closely and trust that your own true voice will guide you into a deeper knowing, a deeper sense of who you are, what matters, and the legacy you're living every moment of your life.

WELCOME! WELCOME HOME

You have crossed a significant threshold. In daring to wear your soul on the outside, you have affirmed the transformative power of your own true voice and said *yes* to the golden life that is waiting just for you. As you continue to live your story, and as the events of your life resound within you, remember to lean in to and listen closely to what your life is telling you. For you are a magnificent work of art, a great masterpiece who must be cared for, tended to, and lifted up.

Even now, you are being supported, buoyed up by a great cloud of witnesses, those who cleared a path and broke new ground for you and your children, those who watch, wait, and cheer you on. As you build the road and construct bridges for others, you must always remember the grand invitation: to be of use, to keep your promises, to show the way as you sing the magnificent song of yourself into the great heart and bosom, the wondrous soul of a waiting world.

> *Sometimes in their chanting, monks will land upon a note and sing it in florid fashion. One syllable of text for fifty notes of chant. Melisma, they call it. Living a melismatic life in imitation of plainchant, we may stop on an experience, a place, a person, or a memory and rhapsodize in imagination. . . . Living one point after another is one form of experience. . . . But stopping for melisma gives the soul its reason for being.*
> THOMAS MOORE

WORKS CITED

Adler, N. Quoted in B. Jensen, *What Is Your Life's Work? Answer the Big Question About What Really Matters . . . and Reawaken the Passion for What You Do.* New York: HarperCollins, 2005.

Arrien, A. *The Second Half of Life: Opening the Eight Gates of Wisdom.* Boulder, Colo.: Sounds True, 2005.

Avery, B. *An Altar of Words: Wisdom, Comfort, and Inspiration for African-American Women.* New York: Broadway Books, 1998.

Basler, R. (ed). *The Collected Works of Abraham Lincoln.* New Brunswick, N.J.: Rutgers University Press, 1953.

Block, P. *Civic Engagement and the Restoration of Community: Changing the Nature of the Conversation.* Cincinnati, Ohio: A Small Group, 2007. Available at http://www.asmallgroup.net.

Brazile, D. Speech delivered at the Linkage, Inc., Women in Leadership Summit, San Francisco, 2007.

Brussat, F., and Brussat, M. *Spiritual Literacy: Reading the Sacred in Everyday Life.* New York: Scribner, 1996.

Buechner, F. *Beyond Words: Daily Readings in the ABCs of Faith.* San Francisco: HarperOne, 2004.

Burgess, G. "Christina's World." In *Journey of the Rose.* Edmonds, Wash.: Jazz Media, 1998.

Burgess, G. "Song to Myself." In *Journey of the Rose.* Edmonds, Wash.: Jazz Media, 1998.

Chisholm, S. Quoted in B. Lanker, *I Dream a World: Portraits of Black Women Who Changed America.* New York: Stewart, Tabori & Chang, 1989.

Chopra, D. *365 Days of Love and Healing*. New York: Workman, 1996.

Cummings, E. "i thank You God for most this amazing." In *XAIPE*. New York: Norton, 1950.

Dass, R., and Gorman, P. *How Can I Help? Stories and Reflections on Service*. New York: Knopf, 1985.

Davidson, S. "Face to Face with Angelina Jolie." *Reader's Digest*, June 2007, pp. 158–164.

DeMille, A. *Martha: The Life and Work of Martha Graham*. New York: Random House, 1991.

DePree, M. *Leadership Is an Art*. New York: Currency Doubleday, 1989.

Dickinson, E. "I Dwell in Possibility." In *The Poems of Emily Dickinson*. Cambridge, Mass.: Belknap Press of Harvard University Press, 1951.

Douglas, B. "Nelson Mandela's Welcome to the City of Glasgow." In *Brave Hearts: New Scots Music, a Narada Collection*. New York: Narada Productions, 1998.

Edelman, M. "Standing Up for Children." In P. Loeb (ed.), *The Impossible Will Take a Little While: A Citizen's Guide to Hope in a Time of Fear*. New York: Perseus, 2004.

Estés, C. *Letter to a Young Activist During Troubled Times*. 2003–2005. Available at http://www.mavenproductions.com/estes.html.

Fahra, S. Quoted in J. Petrina, *Rainier Valley Narrative: Portraits and Stories from the Immigrant and Refugee Communities of Seattle's Rainier Valley*. 2007. Available at http://www.joannepetrina.com/projects/rainier valley/narrative_15.html.

Faulkner, W. Acceptance speech, Nobel Prize in Literature, Stockholm, Sweden, 1950.

Felix, A. *Andrea Bocelli: A Celebration*. New York: St. Martin's Press, 2000.

Fritz, R. *Creating: A Practical Guide to the Creative Process and How to Use It to Create Anything—a Work of Art, a Relationship, a Career, or a Better Life*. Burlington, Mass.: Butterworth-Heinemann, 1995.

Gibran, K. *The Prophet*. New York: Knopf, 1923.

Goleman, D., Kaufman, P., and Ray, M. *The Creative Spirit*. New York: Penguin, 1992.

Goodwin, D. *Team of Rivals: The Political Genius of Abraham Lincoln*. New York: Simon & Schuster, 2005.

Graham, M. *Blood Memory: An Autobiography*. New York: Doubleday, 1991.

Grey, A. *The Mission of Art*. Boston: Shambhala, 1998.

Hayden, R. "Those Winter Sundays." In *Angle of Ascent: New and Collected Poems.* New York: Liveright, 1962.

Hillel the Elder. *Pirkei Avot (Ethics of the Fathers).*

Holy Bible, King James Version. Grand Rapids, Mich.: Zondervan, 2006.

Husband, S. "Profiles." In *Open Book: A Practical Guide for Business Growth.* New York: American Express, 2007.

Ingrasci, R. "Hope for the Fun of It." Unpublished article, 2007.

Jones, A., and O'Neil, J. *Seasons of Grace: The Life-Giving Practice of Gratitude.* Hoboken, N.J.: Wiley, 2003.

Jordan, J. "Poem for South African Women." In *Passion: New Poems, 1977–80.* Boston: Beacon Press, 1980.

Jung, C. *Memories, Dreams, Reflections.* New York: Random House, 1989.

Justice, B., and Justice, R. "Giving Thanks: The Effects of Joy and Gratitude on the Human Body." *Health Leader,* November 20, 2005. Available at http://publicaffairs.uth.tmc.edu/hleader/archive/Mind_Body_Soul/2003/givingthanks-1124.html.

Kafka, F. Quoted in R. May, *The Courage to Create.* New York: Norton, 1994.

King, M., Jr. Quoted in C. Carson (ed.), *The Autobiography of Martin Luther King Jr.* New York: Grand Central Publishing, 2001.

Kirby, J., and Stewart, T. "The Institutional Yes." *Harvard Business Review,* October 2007, pp. 74–82.

Lanker, B. *I Dream a World: Portraits of Black Women Who Changed America.* New York: Stewart, Tabori & Chang, 1989.

Lorde, A. *Sister Outsider: Essays and Speeches.* Freedom, Calif.: Crossing Press, 1984.

Luke, H. "Give Your Unique Gift." In F. Brussat and M. Brussat, *100 Ways to Keep Your Soul Alive: Living Deeply and Fully Every Day.* San Francisco: HarperOne, 1994.

Maathai, W. Nobel lecture, Nobel Peace Prize, Oslo, Norway, 2004.

May, R. *The Courage to Create.* New York: Norton, 1994.

Moore, T. *Meditations: On the Monk Who Dwells in Daily Life.* New York: HarperCollins, 1994.

Murray, A. Quoted in J. Cymbala and D. Merrill, *Fresh Faith.* Grand Rapids, Mich.: Zondervan, 1999.

Nepo, M. *The Book of Awakening: Having the Life You Want by Being Present to the Life You Have.* San Francisco: Red Wheel/Weiser, 2000.

Nerburn, K. *Letters to My Son: A Father's Wisdom on Manhood, Women, Life, and Love.* Novato, Calif.: New World Library, 1999.

Palmer, P. *A Hidden Wholeness: The Journey Toward an Undivided Life.* San Francisco: Jossey-Bass, 2004.

Phillips, J. *Marry Your Muse: Making a Lasting Commitment to Your Creativity.* Wheaton, Ill.: Quest Books, 1997.

Picasso, P. Quoted in R. May, *The Courage to Create.* New York: Norton, 1994.

Piercy, M. "To Be of Use." In *To Be of Use.* New York: Doubleday, 1973.

Roethke, T. "The Waking." In *The Waking: Poems, 1933–1953.* New York: Doubleday, 1953.

Shapiro, R. *Hasidic Tales: Annotated and Explained.* Woodstock, Vt.: SkyLight Paths, 2004.

Shenks, J. *Lincoln's Melancholy: How Depression Challenged a President and Fueled His Greatness.* Boston: Houghton Mifflin, 2005.

Skarmeas, N. *Our Presidents: Their Lives and Stories.* Nashville, Tenn.: Ideals, 1994.

Sontag, S. *Illness as Metaphor.* New York: Farrar, Straus & Giroux, 1978.

South African Women's Freedom Song. Available at http://www .sahistory.org.za/pages/governence-projects/womens-struggle/ introduction.htm.

Teresa, M. Quoted in F. Brussat and M. Brussat, *Spiritual Literacy.* New York: Scribner, 1996.

Vecchione, P. *Writing and the Spiritual Life: Finding Your Voice by Looking Within.* Lincolnwood, Ill.: NTC, 2001.

Walker, M. Quoted in B. Avery, *An Altar of Words: Wisdom, Comfort, and Inspiration for African-American Women.* New York: Broadway Books, 1998.

Wallechinsky, D., and Loucky, J. *The Complete Book of the Olympics.* London: Aurum Press, 2008.

Wesley, J. Quoted in F. Brussat and M. Brussat, *Spiritual Literacy.* New York: Scribner, 1996.

Williams, T. *Red: Passion and Patience in the Desert.* New York: Pantheon Books, 2001.

Williamson, M. *A Return to Love: Reflections on the Principles of* A Course in Miracles. New York: HarperCollins, 1996.

Wise, J. Quoted in *MISys Update Weekly,* MISys, Inc., May 13, 2003.

Zander, R., and Zander, B. *The Art of Possibility: Transforming Professional and Personal Life.* Boston: Harvard Business School Press, 2000.

RESOURCES

These resources are for your ongoing learning. They have been and continue to be helpful to me and to my clients and students. The resources focused on writing will help you whether or not you write, for the spiritual journey is one and the same.

Block, P. *Community: The Structure of Belonging.* San Francisco: Berrett-Koehler, 2008.

Bly, R. (ed.). *The Soul Is Here for Its Own Joy: Sacred Poems from Many Cultures.* Hopewell, N.J.: Ecco Press, 1995.

Brussat, F., and Brussat, M. (eds.). *100 Ways to Keep Your Soul Alive: Living Deeply and Fully Every Day.* San Francisco: HarperOne, 1994.

Burgess, G. *Journey of the Rose.* Edmonds, Wash.: Jazz Media, 1998.

Cameron, J. *The Artist's Way: A Spiritual Path to Higher Creativity.* New York: Tarcher, 1992.

Chalika, J., and Joly, E. (eds.). *Mother Teresa: The Joy in Loving.* New York: Viking, 1997.

Chopra, D. *365 Days of Love and Healing.* New York: Workman, 1996.

Chopra, D. *The Spontaneous Fulfillment of Desire: Harnessing the Infinite Power of Coincidence.* New York: Harmony Books, 2003.

Eldredge, J. *Wild at Heart: Discovering the Secret of a Man's Soul.* Nashville, Tenn.: Nelson, 2001.

Eldredge, J. *Waking the Dead: The Glory of a Heart Fully Alive.* Nashville, Tenn.: Nelson, 2003.

Harrison, L. *Kindred Spirits: Stories, Passions, and Portraits from the Heart of Community.* Anacortes, Wash.: Island Time Press, 2001.

Herman, D., and Black, C. *Spiritual Writing: From Inspiration to Publication.* Hillsboro, Ore.: Beyond Words, 2002.

Hollis, J. *Finding Meaning in the Second Half of Life: How to Finally, Really Grow Up.* New York: Gotham Books, 2005.

Levitt, P. *Fingerpainting on the Moon: Writing and Creativity as a Path to Freedom.* New York: Harmony Books, 2003.

Moon, J. *Stirring the Waters: Writing to Find Your Spirit.* Boston: Journey Editions, 2001.

Moore, T. (ed.). *The Education of the Heart: Readings and Sources for Care of the Soul, Soul Mates, and the Reenchantment of Everyday Life.* New York: HarperCollins, 1996.

Moore, T. *Care of the Soul: A Guide for Cultivating Depth and Sacredness in Everyday Life.* New York: HarperCollins, 1992.

Norris, K. *Amazing Grace: A Vocabulary of Faith.* New York: Riverhead Books, 1998.

O'Donohue, J. *Eternal Echoes: Exploring Our Yearning to Belong.* New York: HarperCollins, 1999.

Palmer, P. *Let Your Life Speak: Listening for the Voice of Vocation.* San Francisco: Jossey-Bass, 1999.

Quinn, R. *Building the Bridge as You Walk on It: A Guide for Leading Change.* San Francisco: Jossey-Bass, 2004.

Spence, L. *Legacy: A Step-by-Step Guide to Writing Personal History.* Athens, Ohio: Swallow Press/Ohio University Press, 1997.

Whyte, D. *The Heart Aroused: Poetry and the Preservation of the Soul in Corporate America.* New York: Doubleday, 1994.

Wilder, B. *Embracing Your Power Woman: Coming of Age in the Second Half of Life.* Boulder, Colo.: Wild Ox Press, 2005.

APPRECIATIONS

I wish to express my deep appreciation for my fellow cultural, corporate, spiritual, social, citizen, and creative artists who wear their souls on the outside, for you have cleared paths, built roads, and constructed bridges for each of us to find our way. Thanks in particular to the following individuals and organizations:

African World Wisdom • Maya Angelou • Angeles Arrien • Christina Baldwin • Melody Beattie • Geoff Bellman • Mary McLeod Bethune • Frederick Buechner • Jeff Bezos • R. B. Blackmon • Peter Block • Andrea Bocelli • Paul Brainerd • Gwendolyn Brooks • Quinn Burgess • Cave Canem • John Carter • Ron Chisholm • Deepak Chopra • Lucille Clifton • Robert Crosby • Max DePree • Meister Eckhart • Marion Wright Edelman • T. S. Eliot • William Faulkner • Nikky Finney • Morgan Freeman • Daniel Goleman • Mary Jane Gillespie • Martha Graham • Alex Grey • Richard Haas • Joye Hardiman • Joy Harjo • Robert Hayden • Terrance Hayes • bell hooks • Langston Hughes • Rick Ingrasci • Angelina Jolie • June Jordan • Martin Luther King Jr. • Coretta Scott King • Brian Lanker • Jacob Lawrence • Jan Levy • Eric Liu • Lee Young-Li • Luz Long • Audre Lorde • Dean L. L. Love • Helen M. Luke • Wangari Maathai • Nelson Mandela • Branford Marsalis • Benjamin Mays • Ruth Mompati • Earnest McEwen Jr. • Mildred McEwen • Thomas Merton • Arnold Mindell • Maxine Mimms • Thomas Moore • Toni Morrison • Bill Moyers • Harold Nelson • Mark Nepo • Pablo Neruda • Kathleen Norris • Henry Nouwen • Naomi Shihab Nye • Barack Obama • John O'Donohue • Georgia O'Keeffe • L. Lamont Okey • Mary Oliver • Barry Oshry • Parker Palmer • Saint Paul • Nicholas Pennell • Gifford Pinchot III • Sidney Poitier • Leontyne Price • Robert Quinn • Michael Ray • Eleanor Roosevelt • Sonia Sanchez • John Scherer • Florida Maxwell Scott • Konji Sebati • Peter Senge • Ntozake Shange • Bill Shore • William Stafford • Sekou Sundiata • Sweet Honey in the Rock • Peggy Taylor • Susan L. Taylor • Mother Teresa • Jackie Torrance • Archbishop Desmond Tutu • Cicely Tyson • Derek Walcott • Frank X. Walker • Evelyn Wemhoff • Marvin Weisbord • David Whyte • Nancy Willard • Serena Williams • Venus Williams • Oprah Winfrey • Benjamin Zander • Rosamund S. Zander

THE AUTHOR

Gloria J. Burgess, Ph.D., is a behavioral scientist, consultant, and executive coach, as well as an award-winning poet, author, director, and performing artist. She has extensive experience as an executive and senior leader, developing leaders and engaging organizations, communities of practitioners, and individuals in finding their vital core and creative genius. Using the motifs of authenticity, creativity, soulful expression, and cultural inclusion, she helps others live their legacy, now and for the future.

A sought-after speaker, Gloria delivers inspirational keynotes for a wide spectrum of audiences, including the South African Embassy; the International Coach Federation; the Providence Health System; the Women's International Network and other global leadership forums; corporate and professional organizations in business, engineering, finance, education, law, health care, human services, hospice, and pastoral care; and various foundations and trusts. Gloria infuses her keynotes and other presentations with poetry and music, artistically employing these universal languages to lift up the human spirit. Sharing her passion for legacy living, authentic leadership, and creativity, Gloria leads retreats for corporate, civic, and charitable organizations throughout the world. She is recognized by the University of Michigan as a Distinguished Scholar in Performing and Directing.

Gloria is the author of the best-selling book *Legacy Living*. Her clients include Microsoft, MSNBC, Boeing, the Girl Scouts of USA, AT&T, Qwest, the International Coach Federation, the Robert Wood Johnson Foundation, the Helene Fuld Trust, the Casey

Family Programs, the Skagit River Poetry Festival, and the Lift Every Voice Foundation. She has taught at her alma maters, the University of Michigan, the University of Southern California, and the Leadership Institute of Seattle (LIOS). She currently teaches at the Bainbridge Graduate Institute, Saybrook Institute, and the University of Washington, where she is an affiliate assistant professor. A Cave Canem Poetry Fellow, Gloria has published several volumes of poetry, including *The Open Door* and *Journey of the Rose*. Her poetry appears in a number of journals and anthologies and has been featured on National Public Radio's *All Things Considered* and British Public Radio.

For more information about Gloria's life-changing story and her keynotes, retreats, performances, books, CDs, and other services and products, contact her at info@gloriaburgess.com, or visit her Web site, www.gloriaburgess.com.

SHARE YOUR BLESSINGS: SEND ME
YOUR PROMISES STORIES

I invite you to share the blessings of your journey with me and with others. If you have a promises story that you would like to share, please visit www.gloriaburgess.com and look for the links to submit your story for possible posting on the Web site; also on this site you can read about others' blessings and stories. By sharing your story with others, you will provide the bread of kindness and encouragement for those who hunger and a cup of insight and joy for those who thirst.

You can also send your promises stories to me via e-mail at promises@gloriaburgess.com.

INDEX